STUDENT PRAYER

SCM PRESS LTD
56 BLOOMSBURY STREET, LONDON WC1

First published 1950

Printed in Great Britain by
Northumberland Press Limited
Gateshead on Tyne

ON PRAYER

Jesus said:

Where two or three are gathered together in my name, there am I in the midst of them.

Seek first the kingdom of God, and his righteousness, and all these things shall be added unto you.

Use not vain repetitions, as the heathen do; for they think they shall be heard for their much speaking.

Ask, and it shall be given you; seek, and ye shall find; knock, and it shall be opened unto you.

In everything, by prayer and supplication, with thanksgiving, let your requests be made known unto God.

St. Paul

Thou hast made us for thyself, and our hearts are restless till they find rest in thee.

St. Augustine

It is permissible to pray for whatever it is permissible to desire.

St. Thomas Aquinas

Prayer is the ascent of mind and heart to God.

St. Hilary

Christian prayer is not an attempt to use God for our purposes, but a petition that he will use us for his.

William Temple

ON PRAYER

Where two or three are gathered together in my name there am I in the midst of them.

Seek ye first the kingdom of God and his righteousness and all these things shall be added unto you.

Use not vain repetitions, as the heathen do; for they think that they shall be heard for their much speaking.

Ask, and it shall be given you; seek, and ye shall find; knock, and it shall be opened unto you.

In everything by prayer and supplication with thanksgiving let your requests be made known unto God.

[illegible]

[illegible] for myself and our hearts [illegible]

[illegible]

[illegible]

[illegible]

[illegible]

CONTENTS

Part III

A Holy People

Part IV

A Treasury of Christian Prayer

TO THOSE WHO USE THIS BOOK

There are three points which it is important to bear in mind about *Student Prayer*: (i) It is not meant to cover every aspect of a student's prayer life, but rather to supplement the regular worship of the Church. (ii) Hardly any of it can be used as it stands; the material mostly requires personal selection and adaptation. (iii) It is an experimental book. Each of these points needs some elaboration.

In the first place *Student Prayer* assumes that Christian students will be taking part in the ordinary worship of the Church, Sunday by Sunday. Students share the virtues and vices of all Christians, and in many ways there is nothing peculiar about them. On the other hand they have their special concerns, as do other groups in the community. Moreover the general problems of living to some extent press upon them in special ways. In the case of students this arises out of the intellectual tasks to which they are committed. Students stand in need of special graces, are prone to special sins, have special occasions for thanksgiving, and are bound to intercede for areas of thought and life which do not come within the experience of most other Christians to anything like the same extent. *Student Prayer* tries to meet the needs of those whose life is lived mainly within the university or college community (at both the senior and junior level) by helping them to relate the intellectual and communal activities which fill most of their waking hours to the central aspects of Christian prayer, and thus to proclaim in worship and action the lordship of Christ over college life. To this end material is provided for both private prayer, less formal occasions of public worship such as S.C.M. branch prayers, and more formal services. The use of this book may also help students to fill out the content of regular Church worship with some specific meanings from their own experience as students. For instance a general confession that "we have left undone those things which we ought to have done, and we have done those things which we ought not to have done" may well include for a student such things as wasting time in the cafeteria, or not having an open mind before the facts of historical research.

Student Prayer, in the second place, is not about prayer, but is a source book of prayers and materials for worship. Hastily reading or using a few pages is not possible with most of it, or profitable with any. It is meant as a guide, and as a stimulation to further exploration of one's own on similar lines. Careful preparation in the selection and arrangement of relevant and good hymns (if hymns are to be used), of Bible passages and of material from Part IV is all necessary. Used in this way the book may well revitalize the prayer life of a Branch.

Those who are accustomed to extemporare prayers should use the book as a source of guidance in the range and content of them. They are a precious heritage in Christendom, to be cherished together with the Church's rich liturgical tradition. It is to be hoped that all Christians will use from time to time that form of prayer with which they are less familiar.

With regard to the actual construction of services, there is a useful treatment in a pamphlet published by the S.C.M. Press, *The Leadership of Corporate Prayer* (price 6d., post free). Suffice it to say here that the main elements of Christian prayer should be included in the structure of acts of worship of any length, though they cannot all be included in shorter periods. They are:

Adoration, in which we praise God for what he is.
Confession, in which we admit our unworthiness.
Thanksgiving, in which we offer thanks for his mercies.
Intercession, in which we ask his blessing for others.
Petition, in which we pray for ourselves.

Thirdly, *Student Prayer* is an experimental book. It had a predecessor, *A Book of Prayers for Students* (now out of print), which was a pioneer in its day and helped many generations of students to enrich their understanding and deepen their experience of Christian prayer. *Student Prayer* in its turn breaks new ground in some respects. Part of the material has already been used effectively by S.C.M. Branches and individual students, but a large amount in the first three sections is entirely new. Faults of omission and commission will become clear by use. Those who have worked together to produce this book will be glad to receive criticisms of their work, which should be sent to the S.C.M. Press. After a few years' trial it is hoped that a thorough revision will both be possible and called for. In the meantime the prayer of the compilers is that in its present form the book will help Christian students of to-day to present their particular vocation to God in prayer, so that all may be done to his glory.

I

THE BIBLE IN WORSHIP

SOME OUTLINES OF BIBLICAL SERVICES

These forms are meant essentially to suggest a *method.* The first three have been worked out in full. For No. 1 Books of Common Prayer or Bibles are required, and for No. 2 copies of this book, sufficient for the company. No. 3 is longer than the others, and can be divided into sections and used, for example, at a week-end conference. The remainder should be capable of being used in a quarter of an hour or twenty minutes at Branch prayers, but can, of course, easily be filled out with additional intercessions, etc., to take twice as long. Nos. 4-6 leave nearly all the work of preparation to be done by the leader.

In all, the important thing is the reading of the Bible passages, and the passing straight on to worship. It is not necessary that there should be many other words; the lines of thought can be filled out with prayers from Part IV or elsewhere, with the leader's own prayers, with biddings, or with silence. It is often effective to have the Bible readings shared among several readers.

All the great doctrines of the Bible can be "prayed through" in this way, both in public and in private. Those who find these specimens useful should construct their own.

(1) The Creation

In the beginning God created the heaven and the earth. And God saw everything that he had made, and behold, it was very good.

Let us hear the words of the Prophet in the 40th Chapter of Isaiah.

Isa. 40. 12-18, 21-26 (or another selection)

or

Let us hear the words of the Lord

Job 38, verses 4-11 and 16 to the end of Chapter 39 (or a selection)

Let us call to mind what we have read and heard of the dimensions of the universe; of the multitude of the stars as the grains of sand upon the sea-shore; and let us worship God who said, Let there be light; and there was light.

Let us say together (or in alternate verses)

Psalm 19. 1-6 *or* Psalm 104. 1-6

Calling to mind what we have heard of the inexhaustible variety and energy of living things—let us worship God who gives life to all life.

Psalm 104. 24-30

What is man, that thou art mindful of him, or the son of man, that thou visitest him? Thou hast made him a little lower than the angels, to crown him with glory and honour.

Let us call to mind the greater wonder, that God has given us eyes to see, and minds to understand; hearts to love, and wills that are free to obey or to rebel:—

Let us worship God, who has made us in his image.

I will give thanks unto thee, for I am fearfully and wonderfully made.

Psalm 139. 1-12 (or part) *or* Psalm 24. 1-6

Let us complete our reading of the 19th Psalm.

Psalm 19. 7-end *or* part of Psalm 119 *or* Mic. 6.8

Let us humbly acknowledge before God that we have not kept his Law. We have not fulfilled the purpose of our Creator, but have sought to take control of our own destiny; we have devastated the earth, and exploited the lower creation. We have lived in fear, and fear has made us cruel. We have sought to be as God, and have fallen lower than the beasts.

Let us remember the state of . . . (Europe, Palestine, the slums in this city) . . . and the dullness and deadness of many people's lives . . . and of our own compared to what they might be . . . and let us acknowledge our share in the responsibility for these things.

Let us remember those who suffer for their own or others' fault and those who suffer for no fault that we can see.

Silence, or a short form of general confession (Part IV, Nos. 20-37) *or* part of Psalm 38 or 51

But as his majesty is, so is his mercy.

Isa. 40. 27-31 *or* Matt. 6. 25-30 *or* Luke 12. 6-7

Thank God that in Christ there is a new creation, and that in Christ all things return to him in whom they had their origin. Thank God that although he does not explain, he does redeem.

Rom. 8. 18-23 (or 25) *or* Rev. 5. 11-14

Pray for all those who in their measure share in the creative work of God . . . (artists, parents, teachers, farmers, industrialists . . . who?).
Pray for those who are called to share in the redemptive work of God . . . (priests, ministers of the gospel . . . all Christians). Pray for those whose surroundings conceal God, whose work denies him . . .; for those who say in their hearts: There is no God. Pray for our own work as students . . . etc. (Further applications *ad lib.*)

General Thanksgiving (Part IV, No. 43)

(2) The Incarnation

V. "Behold, I stand at the door, and knock";
R. Amen, come, Lord Jesus.

1. John 1. 1-16 — His birth in the flesh.
   John 3. 3-8 and 16 — Our birth in the Spirit.

V. O Christ, who wast made flesh, and once didst dwell among us;
R. Dwell in us, now and for ever.

2. John 4. 10-14 — Living Water.
   John 6. 33-35, 51-58 — The Bread of Life.

V. O Christ, who gavest once thy body to be broken, and thy blood to be shed;
R. Nourish us, now and for ever.

3. John 14. 10-13 — The Father's work; Christ's works, and ours.

V. O Christ, who once didst perform thy mighty works among us;
R. Work in us, now and for ever.

4. John 14. 19-24 The Father, Jesus and the disciples, one life, one love.

or *or*

John 14. 16-24 The Father, Jesus, and the Comforter in the disciples.

V. O Christ, who hast promised that thou wilt not leave us comfortless;
R. Abide in us, now and for ever.

5. John 17, esp. 18-26 One consecration, one mission, and one glory.

V. O Christ, who didst sanctify thyself for our sakes;
R. Sanctify us also in truth.
V. O Christ, who art one with the Father;
R. Make us one with thee.
V. O Christ, who art for ever with the Father in glory;
R. Take us to be with thee.

Collect for Christmas II (*B.C.P.* 1928). See Part IV, No. 199.
Collect for Ascension Day. See Part IV, No. 205.
Intercession should include the Church, that wonderful and sacred mystery; claiming for all Christians the promise of the divine indwelling. Penitence should include obstinate clinging to private ideas and ways. Thanksgiving should include the communion of saints. Petition "God be in my head", etc. (See Part IV.)

(3) The Last Things

This needs a longer period than the other services, and the several parts may be used at different times.

"It is a fearful thing to fall into the hands of the living God."

"Eye hath not seen, neither hath it entered into the heart of men to conceive, what good things God hath prepared for them that love him."

The theme of our worship is The Last Things: Death, Judgment, Heaven and Hell. Unless we face the truth of these things, faith loses its depth, history seems purposeless, and we live in a fool's paradise.

DEATH

God is eternal, but we have to die. That is true not only of individuals, but also of nations and civilizations.

Let us read together Psalm 90. 1-12.

Let us acknowledge before God that we have shared in the sins of our time, and have sought happiness in the good things of this life only; we have trusted in the wisdom and skill of mortal man, and not in the eternal God; we have been trivial and superficial in thought and action; we have wasted our time, and have not used our opportunities rightly. We have feared death, we have ignored death. We cannot avoid death; but we have neglected him who has overcome death.

Lord, have mercy upon us.
Christ, have mercy upon us.
Lord, have mercy upon us.

or

In the midst of life we are in death: of whom may we seek for succour, but of thee, O Lord, who for our sins art justly displeased. But spare us, Lord most holy, O God most mighty, O holy and merciful Saviour, thou most worthy Judge eternal, suffer us not, at our last hour, for any pains of death, to fall from thee.

Intercession

For the dying; for the sick, wounded and disabled; for those who die suddenly or unprepared; for little children dying; for those who die in despair, for those condemned to death; for the works of mortal men, in art, in philosophy, in science and in statecraft: that they may reflect the beauty of the Lord our God, and be established by his presence.

Psalm 90. 13-17 *or* Psalm 103. 13-17

AND AFTER DEATH, THE JUDGMENT

Let us hear our Lord's parable of the Last Judgment, and, as we hear it, judge for ourselves where we should stand.

Matt. 25. 31-46

or

Let us hear our Lord's parable about the faithful use of the opportunities given us in this life.

Matt. 25. 14-30

or

Let us hear our Lord's parable of those who becoming careless were taken unprepared.

Matt. 25. 1-13

or (with suitable introduction) one of the following:

Luke 12. 4-10, 16-20, 41-48

Silence

Let us pray.

Remember not, Lord, our offences, nor the offences of our forefathers; neither take thou vengeance of our sins: spare us, good Lord, spare thy people, whom thou hast redeemed with thy most precious blood, and be not angry with us for ever:

Spare us, good Lord.

From all evil and mischief; from sin, from the crafts and assaults of the devil; from thy wrath and from everlasting damnation:

Good Lord, deliver us.

From all blindness of heart; from pride, vainglory, and hypocrisy; from envy, hatred, and malice, and all uncharitableness:

Good Lord, deliver us.

By the mystery of thy holy incarnation; by thy holy nativity and circumcision; by thy baptism, fasting and temptation:

Good Lord, deliver us.

By thine agony and bloody sweat; by thy cross and passion; by thy precious death and burial; by thy glorious resurrection and ascension; and by the coming of the Holy Ghost:

Good Lord, deliver us.

In all time of our tribulation; in all time of our wealth; in the hour of death, and in the day of judgment:

Good Lord, deliver us.

(*from the Litany, B.C.P.*)

Jesus said: Verily, verily, I say unto you, he that heareth my word, and believeth him that sent me, hath eternal life, and cometh not into judgment, but hath passed out of death into life. (John 5. 24.)

Thanksgivings

Let us give thanks:

for all who have performed their duties in life as men and women who wait for their Lord;

for the enrichment to our common life of the faithfulness of those who knew that they lived under God's judgment and by his mercy;

for the assurance that Christ will come again to be our judge; and that we shall all appear before him;

for the knowledge that all things will be summed up in him.

V. Bless the Lord, O my soul;

R. *And all that is within me bless his holy name.*

Intercessions

Let us pray:

for all who have lost their way;

for all who are in danger of losing their true life;

for any who are in danger of rejecting the Holy Ghost;

for those who lead others astray;

for the proud and clever;

for the hopeless and despairing;

for those who shirk their responsibilities.

V. O Lamb of God, that takest away the sins of the world;

R. *Have mercy upon us.*

V. O Lamb of God . . .;

R. *Receive our prayer.*

or Save, Lord, by love or fear.
Collect (Part IV, No. 203).

HELL

Read Matt. 25. 1-13.

Lord, thou hast shown us according to thy holy Word, that they who come to thee shall in no wise be cast out, while those that refuse thy love shall not behold thy face. Grant, we pray thee, that having ever in remembrance our frail condition and our wayward wills, we may use our freedom not to our own condemnation but to thy honour and glory, through Jesus Christ, our Lord.

V. From the despising of thy mercy and the spurning of thy love;
R. Good Lord, deliver us.
V. From pride in our sufficiency and contentment with our ignorance;
R. Good Lord, deliver us.
V. From a rebellious will and all hardening of heart;
R. Good Lord, deliver us.
V. From the refusal of charity and the loneliness of the damned;
R. Good Lord, deliver us.
V. From the darkness of our self-destruction, and the pains of thy absence;
R. Good Lord, deliver us.
V. From hell and from damnation;
R. Good Lord, deliver us.

Let us Pray: Part IV, Nos. 36 and 31.

HEAVEN

Fear not, little flock, it is your Father's good pleasure to give you the kingdom. (Luke 12. 32.)

Beloved, now are we children of God and it is not yet made manifest what we shall be. We know that, if he shall be manifested, we shall be like him, for we shall see him as he is. (I John 3. 2.)

Let us hear the prayer of Jesus for his disciples.

John 17. 13-24

or

Let us read St. John's vision of the Holy City, New Jerusalem.

Rev. 21. 1-7 and 21-27

or

Let us read St. John's vision of the saints in glory.

Rev. 7. 9-17

or

I Cor. 15. 53-57

Praise God for the offer of eternal blessedness to finite and sinful creatures, and pray that we may really desire what he offers. Praise God for the saints, and for all who have completed their course in his faith, fear and love.

Praise God for the vindication of his rule in and beyond history.

Pray that we may be made fit for his company.

Collect for All Saints' Day (Part IV, No. 207) or one of the following: Part IV, Nos. 79, 92; Eph. 3. 14-21 (changing the persons).

(4) God's Answer to Man's Need

Selected verses from:
1. Man's Cry. Isa. 64; Psalms 44; 74.
2. God's Promise. Isa. 9. 2, 6, 7; 11. 1-9. Selected verses from Isa. 40. 3-11; 49. 1-13; 60; 61; Jer. 33. 14-21; Dan. 7. 13-14.
3. God's Answer. Luke 2. 1-7.
4. Man's Reception. Luke 23. 21.
5. The Result. Acts 2. 32, 33, 36.
6. The Meaning. Phil. 2. 5-11.

May be followed by prayer for a like spirit in us; or rather for the same Spirit who is ours in Christ Jesus:

for humility and self-effacement;
for deeper caring;

or by some other application, starting from some point of the world's need.

(5) The Temptation

I. Matt. 4. 1-4	Deut. 8. 1-3	Matt. 6. 31-33 John 4. 31-34 John 6. 30-35
II. Matt. 4. 5-7	Psalm 91. 9-13 Deut 6. 16 with Exod. 17. 2-7	Mark 8. 31-33 Matt. 26. 36-39, 53 John 15. 18 Heb. 12. 1-4
III. Matt. 4. 8-11	Deut. 6. 13	John 12. 31-33 John 18. 33-37 Matt. 27. 27-31 Matt. 28. 16-18

And therefore:

IV. Mark 8. 34-38
Matt. 20. 25-28
I Cor. 10. 1-13

V. The Lord's Prayer

(6) The Holy Trinity

"The Catholic Faith is this; that we *worship* one God in Trinity and Trinity in Unity; neither confounding the Persons, nor dividing the substance."

I. *God is One*
Deut. 6. 4-5; Isa. 6. 1-8; 45. 18-19; Acts 17. 23f.
Exod. 20. 3, leading to *confession* of following other "gods".
Holy, holy, holy, Lord God of Hosts. Heaven and earth are full of thy glory; glory be to thee, O Lord most high.
or verses from Psalms, e.g., Psalm 99. 1, 2, 5.

II. *The Father is God*
(God as Father in the Christian sense hinted at in O.T., e.g., Psalm 103. 13; Hos. 11. 1.)
My Father: Matt. 7. 21; 10. 32-33; 11. 25-27; 25. 34; 26, verses 39, 42, 53; Luke 23, verses 34, 46.
Your Father: Matt. 6, verses 1, 4, 6, 9, 14, 15, 26, 32; 7. 11.
Luke 12. 32 or Matt. 7. 11; leading to confession of worry, etc., and *act of trust*.

III. *The Son is God*
Mark 1. 9-11.

Matt. 12. 27-30; Mark 14. 61-62; John 8. 54-58; 14. 6-11.

John 1. 1-5, 14-18; Rev. 1. 11-18.

John 20. 26-29, or 14. 8-10, or 17. 3, leading to *act of faith* in the Word made flesh.

IV. *The Holy Spirit is God*

Isa. 11. 1-2; 61. 1; Luke 4. 16-21.

John 7. 38-39; 14. 26; 16. 7-14.

Acts 2. 1-4, 16-17; 16. 7; 19. 1-7.

I Cor. 3. 16-17; 12. 1-6.

Prayer for purity, or guidance, or gifts, or for help in prayer.

V. *Three in One and One in Three*

John 14. 15-24; II Cor. 13. 14; Matt. 28. 19.

Only a few of the above passages should be read under each head; other topics for prayer than those given will naturally suggest themselves.

Another act of worship of the Holy Trinity could be based on Rev., chapters 4 and 5. Note that the "Seven Spirits of God" represent the Spirit's manifold activities (cf. Isa. 11. 1-2 and Zech. 4. 10). Rev. also uses "Spirit" (singular) as in 2. 7, etc.

LITANIES BASED ON INCIDENTS IN THE LIFE OF CHRIST

Intercession for others is most wholesome when it is made in the context of our Lord's saving acts, and so within the stream of his power. Else it often tends to be dictatorial, giving God directives as to what we think he ought to do, or merely neurotic, piling up upon other people's needs our own anxieties about their needs.

A useful way to escape from these dangers is to begin, not with others' needs at all, but with our Lord's work: then we can move in our prayer from what he has done to the needs of those for whom he did it. Some incidents in our Lord's life may be taken: the Biblical account of it read: and then any intercessions that seem appropriate to each incident may be made. The leader will, of course, have to prepare it beforehand.

Take, as an example, what are sometimes called the "Five Sorrowful Mysteries" of our Lord.

1. *The Agony in the Garden*. (Read a verse or two from Luke 22. 39-46.)

Let us pray now for all who are in mental conflict. . . . For those in an agony of indecision—about

their future; about some moral problem; about their belief. For those who are tempted; for the weak-willed, for the passionate. For all in despair, the morbid, the hopeless.
"By thine agony and bloody sweat . . ."
Good Lord, deliver us. (Or alternative prayer and response.)

2. *The Scourging at the pillar.* (Matt. 27. 24-26.)
Let us pray for all in pain. For those in hospitals; for those awaiting operations; for those recovering from operations; for those who cannot be operated upon. For those who are persecuted for righteousness' sake. For those who have a long period of suffering before them. For the dying.
Let us pray, too, for the cruel-minded; for those who delight in torture; for those who are brutal to the young and the weak.
"By thy bitter scourging . . ."
Good Lord, deliver us.

3. *The mocking and crowning with thorns.* (Matt. 27. 27-31.)
For those who endure scorn for Christ's sake and the Gospel; for those who are not ashamed to be accounted fools for the Lord's sake.
Let us pray for the intellectually arrogant; for Christians who look down on the simple-minded; for the proud and those who trust in worldly power; for the falsely ambitious; for those who aim at any crown but one of thorns.

"By the mockery of man and thy crowning with thorns . . ."
Good Lord, deliver us.

4. *The condemnation and the carrying of the Cross.* (John 19. 16-17.)

For the innocent condemned; for all suffering from injustice.
For all under sentence, and for those who minister to them; for prisoners, warders and prison chaplains.
For those who carry great burdens in their lives: their own burdens, burdens of guilt, evil habit, poisoned memories; or others' burdens, anxieties, labour, responsibility.
For those who are given a cross to carry, and are afraid.
"By thy carrying of thy cross . . ."
Good Lord, deliver us.

5. *The Crucifixion.* (Luke 23. 44-46.)

For all sinners, for whom Christ died.
For the impenitent; the hard-hearted and callous; the sensual and undisciplined.
For the complacent and self-satisfied; those who are blind to their defects; the pious who have no charity; the thoughtless and inconsiderate.
For the sinful who are trying to be penitent.
For all of us, that we may see our sins as the instruments of Christ's passion; for true penitence; for pardon.
"By thy crucifixion and thy precious death . . ."
Good Lord, deliver us.

The actual intercessions suggested above are only "to start you thinking"; they are freely adaptable to various situations. Some will want to make more specific and personal petitions—they will fit into the scheme just as well, with a little forethought.

Other suggested incidents in our Lord's life, which might make the pattern of a litany, are:

(*a*) *The Holy Family* (five intercessions)

1. The bringing of the good news by Gabriel to Mary: Luke 1. 26-35 (Preaching, etc.).
2. The visitation of Elizabeth by Mary: Luke 1. 39-42 (Neighbourliness, recognition of each other's qualities, etc.).
3. The nativity of our Lord: Luke 2. 1-7 (Humility, etc.).
4. The presentation of our Lord in the Temple: Luke 2. 22-39 (Fulfilment of the Church's mission).
5. The finding of our Lord in the Temple: Luke 2. 41-49 (Study, learning, etc.).

(*b*) *Christ's Miracles of Healing* (five intercessions)

1. The blind man: Mark 8. 22-25, or John 9. 1-7 (Spiritual blindness, etc.).
2. The man sick of the palsy: Mark 2. 3-12 (ineffectual discipleship, etc.).
3. The man possessed with devils: Mark 5. 2-18 (Wild temper, or neuroses, etc.).
4. The woman with an issue of blood twelve years: Mark 5. 25-34 (Fixed evil habits, the lone individual lost in the crowd but known to God, etc.).

5. The young man raised from the dead: Luke 7. 11-16 (New life to dead souls, etc.).

These are only a few out of the many possible ideas. All that is needed is a Bible, used with sympathy and imagination.

PATER NOSTER

"When ye pray, say Our Father . . ."

The uses of the Lord's Prayer are inexhaustible. It may be used corporately to sum up a number of acts of adoration, confession, intercession or petition. It may be repeated privately a number of times with special intentions, persons, causes, in mind. It may be used as the basis for meditation. Rarely is it possible to cover the whole prayer in a led meditation. Sections of the following meditation might be used as a basis for an act of worship, or as a part of a longer service.

OUR FATHER

Whom we know only through thy Son,
God and Father of Jesus Christ,
creator of all that is,
whose mystery no finite mind can fathom,
thee we adore.

Father of those dear to us,
those who have wronged us,
those who vex us and try our patience,
the homeless, the interned and the prisoners
all who have been made thy sons through Jesus Christ,

all who in every land in diverse tongues offer to thee
the Lord's Prayer,
thee we adore.

WHICH ART IN HEAVEN

Thou art—
the everlasting *I am*,
in whom all things exist,
eternal source of truth and goodness,
beyond and above all existences,
thou art.
Thou who art in heaven,
whose ways are not our ways,
before whose eternity our little lives are as flowers that fade,
from whose eternity they take their worth and meaning,
whose mercy is unfailing,
whose truth endures to all generations.

HALLOWED BE THY NAME

In the return of mankind from the far country to its true home,
the restoring to men of their lost knowledge of thyself,
in a recovered experience of their dependence on thee,
a new reverence for nature as thy creation,
a new understanding that as thy children all men are brethren,
hallowed be thy name.

When thou remainest hidden,
when darkness is over the earth,
when the heavens are silent and life is a hell,
when men cry to thee in vain,
help us to believe in thy name.

In our willing submission to thy judgment,
  our acceptance of the discipline of suffering,
  our learning to live as thy sons,
  the enlargement of our understanding,
  our patience, endurance and hope,
  our growing likeness to the mind of Christ,
    hallowed be thy name.

THY KINGDOM COME

For the prophets who foretold the coming of thy kingdom,
for its descent upon earth in Jesus Christ,
  his revelation of the Father,
  his life-giving words,
  his historic creative deeds,
for the fragmentary realizations of thy kingdom in human history,
  shafts of light that shine through present darkness,
  the transfiguration of our common life by acts of heroism, endurance and kindness,
    we give thee thanks.
Thy kingdom come,
  in the submission of nations and governments to thy laws,
  the honouring of the family,

the restoration of a sense of vocation to work,
the right use of the resources of the earth,
the rekindling of a passion for truth,
the opening of springs of mercy and compassion,
thy reign over every thought, affection and impulse of our being.

THY WILL BE DONE

In thy will is our peace,
in the doing of thy will is our fulfilment and our joy.
In the restoring and perfecting of the world thou hast created,
the quickening of the forces of life,
the affirmation of righteousness,
the growth of understanding, harmony and unity,
thy will be done on earth.
The son of man came to seek and to save that which is lost,
to save the individual whom we love,
to save and redeem mankind,
thy will be done on earth as it is in heaven.

GIVE US OUR DAILY BREAD

From thee we have our life and all that we possess.
Forgive us our pride and self-sufficiency,
teach us to reverence the earth which
thou hast made fruitful,
teach us our oneness with those by whose labour our food is produced and brought across the sea and land.

Thou, who hast made us men, so that we live not by
  bread alone but by thy Word,
feed us this day with the words of life.
Let all that is divine in thy world, let the
  unsleeping power of truth and love,
  possess us and work through us.
Thou art thyself our life,
live in us this day.

FORGIVE, AS WE FORGIVE

As we forgive—
we are but men, O God,
thou art in heaven and we upon earth,
dost thou demand that we be perfect as thou art
  perfect?
With men it is impossible, but not with God.

Teach us to hate, as thou dost hate,
  the cruelty of the oppressor,
  contempt of truth,
  lust of power and sinful pride
  in others or in ourselves.
Take from us the weakness of resentment and revenge,
give us the capacity to understand,
let us not include the guilty and the innocent in a
  single condemnation,
make us partakers of thy infinite pity,
make us content to leave judgment to thee, the all-
  seeing judge of all.

Forgive us our trespasses as we forgive those that
  trespass against us.

Forgive us the egoism which belongs to our nature,
  the sin which is entwined with the roots of our being,
  the unforgivingness of our hearts,
  the blindness which hides from us our need to be forgiven.
Open our eyes to the wonder of thy forgiveness.
Let it inspire in us a forgiveness which can undo the evil in the world and make atonement for men's sins.

LEAD US NOT INTO TEMPTATION, BUT DELIVER US

Darkness is over the earth.
Out of the darkness,
  the confusion and perplexity of our time,
  the vanity of human existence,
  the struggle with forces that threaten to crush the spirit of man,
  we cry unto thee.

Let us not tempt thee by demanding that thou prove thyself God,
let us know that, whatever happens,
  thou art God and our Father.

Let us not be overcome by evil,
let not hope die or courage fail.
Deliver us from the fears and faithlessness of our own hearts,
in the secret places of our souls enable us to believe in thee,

make us in all these things more than conquerors,
through him that loved us.

Deliver us from the evil which infects our time,
from the cynicism and despair,
all forms of self-deception,
the over-simplification of moral issues,
insensitiveness to human needs,
reluctance to take responsibility.

If the days of tribulation may not be shortened,
if we must walk through the dark valley,
if earthly supports fail us,
hold us in thy keeping,
assure us that neither life nor death can separate us
from thy love in Christ Jesus our Lord.

FOR THINE IS THE KINGDOM, THE POWER AND THE GLORY

Thou art sovereign Lord,
sovereign over all the earth.
O Lord, in thee have we trusted,
let us never be confounded.

From The Christian News-Letter (adapted)

II

STUDENT WORSHIP

THE OFFERING OF ACADEMIC WORK

THE HOMAGE OF THE CREATED WORLD

(Man is the priest of creation; as such he is called to voice the homage of the created world to God, both by word, and also by his work in and with these created things. In this service we use an ancient hymn as the vehicle of our priesthood to all the subjects of university study.)

Readings: Gen. 1. 26-28, 31; Dan. 1. 3ff.; I Kings 3. 1-14, and 4. 29-end; Job 28. 20-28; Job 38. 4-7; Rev. 4. 8-11 (one or more may be used).

Approach: *R. Have mercy upon us.*

O God the Father, of heaven, Who didst create and dost sustain the whole created world: *R.*

O God the Son, who wast agent in the creation of the world, and workest to redeem it from corruption: *R.*

O God the Holy Spirit, who at creation didst move upon the face of the waters, bringing order out of chaos, and light out of darkness, and still movest in the hearts of men to sanctify them in truth: *R.*

O holy, blessed and glorious Trinity, three Persons and One God, ever creating, ever redeeming, ever perfecting the world: *R.*

(The following sections may be used singly or in any conjunction.)

I. Let us offer the homage of the spiritual agents of God; the homage of the universe itself, of space and its limits, of the unseen energies of God, of the planets and their courses. In this act we offer the homage of theologians, astronomers and mathematicians.

R. Praise him, and magnify him for ever.

O all ye works of the Lord, bless ye the Lord: *R.*
O ye angels of the Lord, bless ye the Lord: *R.*
O all ye powers of the Lord, bless ye the Lord: *R.*
O all ye heavens, bless ye the Lord: *R.*
O ye waters that be above the firmament, bless ye the Lord: *R.*
O ye sun and moon, bless ye the Lord: *R.*
O ye stars of heaven, bless ye the Lord: *R.*

Glory be to the Father, and to the Son and to the Holy Ghost.
R. As it was in the beginning, is now and ever shall be, world without end.

II. Let us offer the homage of the elements, the climate, the seasons, the ordered sequence of time. In this we offer the homage of those who study geography, meteorology, and physics.

O all ye works of the Lord, bless ye the Lord: *R.*
O ye showers and dew, bless ye the Lord: *R.*
O ye winds of God, bless ye the Lord: *R.*
O ye fire and heat, bless ye the Lord: *R.*

O ye winter and summer, bless ye the Lord: *R.*
O ye frost and cold, bless ye the Lord: *R.*
O ye ice and snow, bless ye the Lord: *R.*
O ye nights and days, bless ye the Lord: *R.*
O ye light and darkness, bless ye the Lord: *R.*
O ye lightnings and clouds, bless ye the Lord: *R.*
Gloria.

III. Let us offer the homage of the earth, and all that lies on and beneath it: soil, vegetable nature, countryside, minerals and chemicals. In this we offer the homage of those studying geology, chemistry, mechanics, engineering, botany, agriculture and forestry.

O all ye works of the Lord, bless ye the Lord: *R.*
O let the earth bless the Lord: *R.*
O ye mountains and hills, bless ye the Lord: *R.*
O all ye green things upon the earth, bless ye the Lord: *R.*
O ye springs (wells), bless ye the Lord: *R.*
O ye seas and floods, bless ye the Lord: *R.*
Gloria.

IV. Let us offer the homage of the animal creation, and of man in his physical nature. In this we offer the homage of those who study zoology, anatomy, physiology, etc.

O all ye works of the Lord, bless ye the Lord: *R.*
O all ye that live and move in the waters, bless ye the Lord: *R.*

O all ye fowls of the air, bless ye the Lord: *R.*
O all ye beasts and cattle, bless ye the Lord: *R.*
O ye children of men, bless ye the Lord: *R.*
Gloria.

V. Let us offer the homage of mankind. In this we offer the homage of all leaders of thought, in art, philosophy, history, languages, science, the Church, education, law, economics, medicine, politics; and finally all who stand alone and suffer in the cause of truth.

O all ye works of the Lord, bless ye the Lord: *R.*
O ye children of men, bless ye the Lord: *R.*
O ye priests of the Lord, bless ye the Lord: *R.*
O ye servants of the Lord, bless ye the Lord: *R.*
O ye spirits and souls of the righteous, bless ye the Lord: *R.*
O ye holy and humble men of heart, bless ye the Lord: *R.*
O Ananias, Azarias, and Misael, bless ye the Lord: *R.*
Gloria.

Selection of Prayers which may follow:

For true judgment: Part IV, No. 206.
For a right spirit of research: Part IV, No. 121 or 117.
Against the temptations involved in our work: Part IV, No. 122.
For all universities and colleges: Part IV, No. 182, 183 or 185.
For growth in faith: Part IV, No. 93, 96 or from 130-135.

Thou art worthy, O Lord, to receive glory and honour and power; for thou hast created all things and for thy pleasure they are, and were created.

THE HUMANITIES
"MAN AS A FREE SPIRIT"

Adoration. Prov. I. 20-23.

Glory be to thee, O Father everlasting, who art creator of all and fountain of truth.

Glory be to thee, O Lord Jesus Christ, who hast brought the light of the gospel to our darkness.

Glory be to thee, O Holy Spirit, who dost inspire in us such a desire of truth as will not let us rest short of the knowledge of God.

Blessed be thou, Father, Son and Holy Spirit, one God; and blessed be thy glorious name for ever.

Confession

Almighty and most merciful Father, we confess in the sight of the whole company of heaven that we have sinned against thy love and against thy truth. Neither with heart, nor soul, nor strength, have we loved our neighbour as ourselves. Above all to-day we confess that we have not loved thee with our minds. We have not owned thy lordship in our thinking. Grant us, most merciful Father, pardon, absolution and remission of this and all our sin, and give us grace to love thee as we ought. Through Jesus Christ, our Lord.

Supplication

Teach us, O God, the love that is revealed in Jesus

Christ, that we may be instructed into thy kingdom of heaven. Grant us the graces of humility and of an enquiring mind, and by thy Spirit guide us into all truth. Lord, we seek to share in the passion of the mind of Christ: give us grace that we, bearing in our minds the division and sin of the world, may know in Christ the redemption wherein all things are made one. This we ask in the name of our Lord Jesus Christ, who taught us when we pray to say:
Our Father . . .

Reading: Wisdom 6; Prov. 8; Ecclus. 30; or 38. 24-39. 15; or 51. 13-22; Job 28. 12-28; or I Cor. 1. 18-25, etc.

Thanksgiving

Lord, we give thee thanks:
for our calling to serve thee in the university (college);
for the subjects that thou hast given us for study;
for the spirit of truth that thou hast sent into the world;
and above all for the death of thy Son upon the cross, and his glorious resurrection wherein thou hast shown thy foolishness to be wiser than the wisdom of men;
grant us minds and hearts to praise thee, and make us ever thankful for all thy blessings. Through Jesus Christ our Lord.

(Here may follow Thanksgivings and Intercessions for one of the faculty subjects below.)

(1) Philosophy

Thanksgiving

Lord, we thank thee for all the wisdom of the past; for the devoted labours of sages and thinkers who have prized truth above all things; for the discipline of clear thinking, and the dissipation of confusion and prejudice.

R. We thank thee, O Lord.

Intercession

Let us lay before God the needs of those who study philosophy.

Almighty God, Father of all mercies, grant us, we pray thee, the love of truth for Christ's sake; teach us to care more for truth than for systems, or for skill in debate; and give us the grace and patience to keep open those questions which philosophy cannot answer.

V. With thee is the fount of life;
R. In thy light shall we see light.

(Here appropriate readings may be added for different departments: e.g.
For those who study logic and epistemology: I Cor. 2. 11-16; or Matt. 11. 25.
For those who study metaphysics: Acts 7. 49-50; Job 38. 4-7; Col. 2. 1-13.
For those who study ethics: Matt. 5. 43-45; Phil. 2. 1-11.

For those who study æsthetics: Ecclus. 38; Matt. 6. 26-30; Phil. 4. 8-9.)

The *V*. and *R*. after each.

For the particular needs of the Philosophy Department in this university (college); for those who teach, and those who learn: *V*. and *R*.

(2) Classics

Thanksgiving

Lord, we thank thee for the traditions of past generations and cultures; for noble literatures and profound teachings; for great lives and generous wills; for all who outside thy covenant yet glimpsed something of thy truth.

R. We thank thee, O Lord.

Intercession. Read Gal. 3. 24.

Bless, O Lord, we beseech thee, the intellectual discipline of classical studies, and teach us to see thy providence in the world into which our Lord was born.

(For those who study Ancient History: Rom. 2. 12-16.

For those who study Classical Literature and Civilization: I Cor. 1. 20-25.

For those who study Greek and Roman Religion: Acts 14. 8-18.)

For the particular needs of the department of Classics in this university (college); for those who teach and those who learn, we humbly pray.

V. and *R*. as before.

(3) Literature

Thanksgiving

Let us thank God for his gifts of poets and writers. For those who have scorned delights and lived laborious days, in poverty and isolation, at the call of letters. For all excellence of impression and communication of insight. For all challenge to frivolity and all deepening of wisdom.

R. We thank thee, O Lord.

Intercession. Read Gen. 1. 1-5; Psalm 148. 5.

Let us pray for all who read and write literature: Part IV, No. 190.

Let us pray for all members of Literature Schools (Faculties, Depts.): for those who teach and those who learn.

V. Thy word is a lantern unto my feet;

R. And a light unto my paths.

For a sense of vocation in letters; for craftsmanship in words; for careful scholarship and for sound judgment: *V.* and *R.*

For a new understanding of thy creation and redemption in all that we read and write, and for guidance in the use of it, that it may be to thy glory: *V.* and *R.*

Let us pray that the beauty of words may be seen as the beauty of holiness, and that the enrichment of experience may deepen our wisdom; through him who came to us, the wisdom and the word of God, Christ Jesus our Saviour, who with the Father and the Holy Ghost liveth and reigneth, one God, world without end.

(4) Education

Thanksgiving

For the discipline of the intellect:

R. We thank thee, O God.

For the discoveries and insights of the mind, and for the satisfaction of truth achieved: *R.*

For the skills imparted to us, and for the fruit of our endeavours: *R.*

Intercession. Read Matt. 13. 51-52; Mark 10. 13-15; etc.

That we may remember that all learning lies under God and only has meaning in his purpose:

R. Hear us, good Lord.

That we may know to what end we learn: *R.*

That we may know how to learn, and thereby how to teach: *R.*

That wisdom, as well as information and skill, may be imparted in our schools: *R.*

That the Christian faith may be taught in them: *R.*

For all in the Education Department of the university (college): *R.*

For teachers called to put theory into practice: *R.*

For teachers overburdened with work and crowded classes: *R.*

For children: that their teachers may not cause them to stumble: *R.*

For thy forgiveness to those who, working in the field of education, have acquiesced in a system that they could not approve: *R.*

For thy forgiveness to teachers (ourselves) when they (we) have given way to impatience toward those with whom they (we) have to deal: *R.*

(5) Psychology

Thanksgiving

For the deeper understanding of the mind and instincts of man:

R. We thank thee, O God.

For the shattering of our pride, and the humility that comes from perceiving our share in the deep instinctive forces of all creation: *R.*

For the healing of the lunatic and possessed, for the dispersal of neurosis and obsession: *R.*

Intercession. Read Luke 8. 26-39; Mark 7. 14-23; or Luke 9. 28-43.

That we may ever remember those committed to our care, not as cases but as persons, not as abstract mental diseases but as creatures and children of thine.

R. Hear us, good Lord.

That we may not use our knowledge as power, but with self-effacement and love: *R.*

For psychiatrists and psychologists: *R.*

For non-Christian practitioners that God may use their skill in spite of their convictions: *R.*

For the conversion of agnostic or atheistic psychologists and students: *R.*

THE SCIENCES
"MAN AS THE LEADER OF CREATION"

Adoration

Psalm 8; or Gen. I. 26; or selections from the Benedicite.

Almighty and eternal God, blessed and holy Trinity, for thine own self:

V. We praise thee;
R. Thine, Lord, is the glory.

Thou source of knowledge, fountain of learning, very truth of truth: *V*. and *R*.

Thou creator of heaven and earth, maker and renewer of physical matter, breathing life into all things living, both plants and animals: *V*. and *R*.

Thou creator and redeemer of man, whom thou willest to have dominion over the earth, and to have communion with thee: *V*. and *R*.

Confession

Let us confess our sins before God.

In imagining that we were lord of truth, and treating knowledge as a source of power to be grasped at for our own ends:

R. O Lord, we have sinned against thee.

In our light acceptance of all created things, and in forgetting that through all the ages thou hast worked to bring the universe to this hour that we might know it: *R*.

In lacking reverence for life, and in denial of our stewardship over living things: *R*.

In our impatience of following the pattern of thy creation, and in imposing our own ideas instead of thy command: *R.*

In forgetting that all spiritual gifts, even the perception of truth, are worthless without the gift of grace: *R.*

In our attempts to fit persons into a scheme of thought derived from our knowledge of things: *R.*

(Here may follow either the following general thanksgiving and intercession, or one of those given on pages 59-60.)

Thanksgiving

For the lower levels of creation, which show forth thy glory, and for our commission to understand them and to be their stewards:

R. We thank thee, O God.

For thy guidance of our predecessors, and for the store of knowledge and of skill which they have passed on to us: *R.*

For the satisfaction which we find in the study of created things, in the method of experiment, and in the discovery of truth: *R.*

For the wonder of the universe, the orderliness and fascination of the natural world, as we stand in reverence before thy creation and in awe before thee: *R.*

But above all we thank thee for the gift of thy Son, in whom thou hast finally revealed thyself, and in whom we have the key to all knowledge of thee and of thy world: *R.*

Intercession

For a right sense of stewardship, because by it we share the provision of God for men:

V. Lord, we believe;
R. Help thou our unbelief.

For interest in our study; for reverence for our subject; for perseverance and steadfastness: *V*. and *R*.

For responsibility in the knowledge and use of scientific invention: *V*. and *R*.

For research scientists, that their isolation may never blind them to life as unified in Christ our Lord: *V*. and *R*.

For the employment of our knowledge for the well-being of men; that whatever we discover or make of our materials we may use with reverence for the purposes of God: *V*. and *R*.

For humility in our learning, and frankness to acknowledge that ours is but one of many avenues of knowledge, not the only one nor yet the most important; and for grace to remember that knowledge does not itself make perfect: *V*. and *R*.

For watchfulness that we become not slaves to our techniques, methods or machines: *V*. and *R*.

(Here may be added thanksgiving and intercessions from the sections for separate faculty subjects below, 1 and 2.

Here also may be added petition:
for a right attitude towards our study;
for the intellectual virtues;
for the community of learning in this place.

See Part IV, Nos. 113-125 and Nos. 182-189.)

(1) Agriculture

Thanksgiving

For our privilege of stewardship over animals and plants:

R. We thank thee, O God.

For the wisdom that grows from the experience we inherit: *R.*

For the speed and economy, and for the more abundant yield that comes from greater technical knowledge and equipment: *R.*

For thy constant lesson that our control is limited, and that we depend on thee who givest the increase: *R.*

Intercession. Read Gen. 1. 24-30; Gen. 2. 19-20.

For all whose work is unsatisfying; for those whose minds and souls are deadened through exhaustion and overwork.

R. We beseech thee, O Lord.

For the maintenance or renewal of rural communities, on the farm and in the village: *R.*

For a right scale of values in the use of machinery and men: *R.*

For the marriage of work and worship, and for a true sense of the place of agriculture in the design of God: *R.*

(2) Applied Science

Thanksgiving

For the marvels of science:

R. We thank thee, O God.

For the lightening of drudgery: *R.*
For the release of power, and the satisfaction of men's needs: *R.*

Intercession. Read I Kings 6. 11-14.
Let us pray for all who study engineering (*or* . . .) that they may understand the materials they use, and the purpose for which they use them.

R. We beseech thee, O Lord.

That in learning to handle the inanimate things of creation, they may never be tempted to handle men as if they were but stone and steel: *R.*
That they may not be lost amidst the detail and techniques of their work, but may ever labour to the benefit and not the danger of man: *R.*
That as Christ through obedience and suffering was made perfect, they may through their acceptance of monotony and routine bring forth order and well-being to man: *R.*
That they themselves, shaped by the creative hand of God, may never rest content with anything but the best that their craftsmanship can achieve: *R.*
Let us pray: O God, who hast made man to be both steward of thy creation and priest to draw out thy purpose for the materials of the earth; so guide by thy Holy Spirit the minds and hearts of thy servants that they may fulfil thy will and promote the well-being and order of mankind; through him who laboured at a carpenter's bench, and came to redeem the whole of life, Jesus Christ our Lord.

SOCIAL STUDIES
"MAN AS A SOCIAL BEING"
History, Law, Economics, Political Theory, Sociology, Commerce, etc.

(This section is not fully worked out, since much of "The Humanities" and "The Sciences" will apply and may be used as a general introduction to "Social Studies".)

Reading: I Cor. 12. 14-26.

Thanksgiving

Let us thank God for the knowledge achieved by scholars in . . . (History, Law, Economics, etc.)

R. Thanks be to God.

For the wisdom of the past to control the impetuous: *R.*

For the better understanding of human relationships: *R.*

For the humility that comes from learning our limitations: *R.*

For the lessons of courage and endurance, of sympathy and good temper, of perseverance and the resilience of man's spirit: *R.*

For the assurance that thy mercy will not forsake mankind, and for the promise of thy blessed hope: *R.*

Intercession

Let us pray for all students of . . . (History, Law, Economics, etc.)

R. We beseech thee to hear us, good Lord.

Let us pray for accuracy: *R.*
For thoroughness: *R.*
For impartiality: *R.*
For sympathy and insight: *R.*
For justice: *R.*
For gratitude to tradition: *R.*
For a responsible awareness of future generations: *R.*
Let us pray: O God, who hast made us members one of another in the family of mankind, and hast submitted us to the laws of mutual dependence; grant that in our studies (of . . .) we may not lose our sympathy; that in the meeting of person with person we may perceive the type of thy presence unto us. Bring all men to the knowledge of thee, and of each other in thee: that we may all be bound together in the bundle of life with thee, O Lord our God.

A MEDITATION ON ROMANS 12. 1-21

(This may also be used, with suitable transposition and responses, as a general intercession for the renewal of the mind.)

Read I Cor. 14. 15.

Lord, thy word endureth for ever.

It giveth light and understanding to the simple.

The fear of the Lord is the beginning of wisdom, blessed is the man that feareth the Lord.

Reading: Romans 12. 1-21.

V. Offer unto God the sacrifice of thanksgiving;

R. And pay thy vows unto the most highest.

We would offer thee the praise of our lips: Part IV, Nos. 39, 42, 43, or 50.

Rom. 12. 1-3.

We would present our bodies a living sacrifice:

That it may please thee to grant us health and vigour and that thou wouldest make our bodies temples meet for thy indwelling.

That it may please thee to give us the gifts of sleep and rest, that our bodies being refreshed they may be the active partners of our spirits.

Prayer: Part IV, No. 112.

We would worship God with minds transformed by his renewing:

That we lack not honesty in doubts and perplexity.
That we lack not accuracy in scholarship and research.
That we may collaborate with others in the search for truth, and may never for popularity or riches turn aside from our task.
We would worship God in proving what is his will, in doing what is good and acceptable and perfect in his sight:
That we may bring all our studies under the good hand of God.
That we may see all things in relation to God, the giver of all truth.
That we may not rest in contemplation of the truth, but may perform it.
That we may bring all thoughts and imaginations into captivity to Christ.

Rom. 12. 3-8.
Let us pray for humility before the truth.
That we may acknowledge our insignificance in his sight.
That in the enthusiasm of our tasks we may not magnify our own importance.
Let us pray for the spirit of co-operation, and the due subordination of every part to him who is the head of the body.
That our own gifts may be used for the glory of God as our service of the Church, in the university of which we are members.
Let us pray for all according to their gifts:
Prophecy. For all called to have insight into the

purposes of God and the ends which man must serve. All with a passion for justice and humanity. Students of political and social theory, theologians and philosophers, historians and writers. All of us in so far as we are called upon to read the signs of the times.

Practical Service (" ministry "). All social scientists, medical students, students of agriculture, engineering, mining and technology. The administrative and domestic staffs. Members of committees, S.R.C., Union. For all of us in our call to citizenship.

Teachers. Professors and lecturers, students of education, S.C.M. staff, study group leaders, all engaged in the teaching ministry of the Church. All called to teach by their example and self-dedication.

Speakers (" exhortation "). S.C.M. Secretary, college chaplain, tutors. The ministry of counsel in the Church. All of us called upon to advise, befriend, sympathize.

Contributors (" he that giveth "). Benefactors to the university. The state that it may support with responsibility and flexibility. Industry that it may not dominate learning through its endowment. Senior friends and supporters of S.C.M. All of us in our serious duty of almsgiving.

Superintendents (" he that ruleth "). All training for leadership in society, politics, local government, or industry. Those preparing to be leaders in the Church. The rector, heads of departments, heads of colleges, wardens of halls, president of S.C.M. and university societies; president of S.R.C. and Union.

Rom. 12. 9-21.
That the love of God may inform all our thinking and acting, enable us to shun all evil and to rejoice in all that is of good report.
That in shyness we may not withdraw from the many.
That we may make an effort to know others and especially all Christians, those who are lonely or distressed and need our friendship.
That we may honour each other in our different denominations, traditions and backgrounds, our different faculties and outlooks.
That we may not shun the meanest tasks that minister to thy glory.
That we may never wilfully flout public opinion or become a reproach to the heathen.

Part IV, Nos. 80 and 85.

A PUBLIC SERVICE

For use on special occasions in the life of a university or college

It is not possible to suggest one service which would be of use in a very great variety of circumstances. There are two rules to be observed in constructing such a service: the effects used should be bold; and the structure simple. This is particularly important if more than one person is taking part in the conduct of the worship.

A Suggested Order of Service

LET US WORSHIP GOD

Hymn: (e.g. All people that on earth do dwell).

Sentences (all still standing): Prov. 2. 6-8; or other suitable passage.

Prayers: Here use may be made of a Bidding Prayer constructed for the occasion, followed perhaps by a few short prayers of Adoration or Thanksgiving (Part IV, Nos. 10, 11, 15, 18 or 38), and Confession (Part IV, Nos. 23, 25, 27) or simply by the repetition of the General Thanksgiving (Part IV, No. 43), the General Confession (Part IV, No. 21) and/or the Lord's Prayer.

Readings: Prov. 8; Wis. 7. 15-end; 9. 1-11; Ecclus. 39. 1-11; 44. 1-15; Mark 12. 28-34; Matt. 6. 19-34; John

9. 1-12, 35-41; Acts 17. 16-31; Rom. 12. 1-8 or 1-21; I Cor. 1. 18–2. 16 or 1. 26–2. 5; Eph. 3. 14-21; Col. 1. 9-23; II Peter 1. 1-11; Rev. 21. 1-7.

If more than one reading is chosen, the Te Deum or some suitable hymn (e.g. Lord, thy word abideth) may be sung between the readings. If there is more than one reader, it should be clearly understood beforehand which introductory and closing words are to be used. There are several possible ways of announcing the reading: "Here beginneth the . . . verse of the . . . chapter of the book of (or Gospel according to) . . . (or Epistle of . . . to . . .)"; "Hear the Word of God as it is contained in (the name of the book) reading at (chapter and verse)"; or simply announce the name of the book, give its chapter and verse. At the end may be added: "Here endeth the lesson"; "May God bless to us the reading of his Holy Word"; or "Thanks be to God".

Hymn: (e.g. A hymn of praise, such as, Praise my soul the King of heaven; or of preparation for hearing the Word of God preached, such as, Come, Holy Ghost, our hearts inspire.)

Sermon

Hymn

Prayers: Petitions and Intercessions (see Part IV, appropriate sections).

Hymn

Blessing

THE CHURCH OVERSEAS

Sentence: Heb. 1. 1 and 2 *or* Mal. 1. 11.

Adoration

Blessed be thou, O God, who hast declared that it is thine eternal purpose to gather in one all things in Christ. Worthy art thou to receive honour and power and glory, for the great love wherewith thou hast loved all mankind and hast delivered us from the powers of darkness and brought us into the kingdom of thy Son.

Reading (e.g. Matt. 28. 16-20; John 21. 15-18; or Acts 11. 1-18)

Thanksgiving

Let us give thanks for the reign of Christ.

For the first disciples who were sent forth to proclaim the coming of the kingdom, for the apostles who carried the gospel to many lands, for those who in dark ages kept alive the light, steadfast under persecution and unwavering in distress.

V. Let us bless the Lord;
R. Thanks be to God.

or

V. Bless the Lord, O my soul;
R. And all that is within me, bless his holy name.

For the witness of the Church in this land, for its

word of judgment and its word of hope to every generation; and, in our own day, for the awareness of sin in its divisions: *V.* and *R.*

For those who have gone to other lands with the news of Christ, for men zealous to bring the light of the gospel to all the world: *V.* and *R.*

That there is now no land where Christ is not worshipped. For the growth of the churches of Asia and Africa, for the treasures of devotion and the riches of understanding which they are bringing into the fellowship of the whole Church. For divine gifts to the Church throughout all the ages: *V.* and *R.*

Confession

Lord, we confess that thy Church is a divided body, no fit instrument for revealing thee to the world.

V. Lord, have mercy;
R. Lord, forgive.

Lord, we confess that as thy Church has been slow to proclaim thee to the nations, so we have failed to pass on to others the love and mercy which we have received in thy Son: *V.* and *R.*

Lord, we confess our indifference to the coming of thy kingdom: we have not waited patiently, or prayed believingly, or given costingly: *V.* and *R.*

In penitence we confess our sin; with hope we recall the promises of forgiveness and the assurances of pardon: "Though your sins be as scarlet they shall be white as snow, though they be red like crimson they shall be as wool.

"The wages of sin is death, but the gift of God is eternal life through Jesus Christ."

Act of Faith

Let us make an act of faith:

in God the Father, whose word will not return unto him void but will accomplish that whereto he sends it;

in God the Son, the head of our race, the second Adam in whom we live;

in God the Holy Spirit, not leaving himself without a witness in any time or place;

in the holy catholic Church, built upon prophet and apostle, Jesus Christ being the chief corner stone: the Church, against which the gates of hell shall not prevail.

V. Lord, we believe in thee;
R. *Help thou our unbelief.*

Intercession

Let us pray for the Church:

for the restoration of her unity; and for all who seek that unity, by prayer, by discussion, through administration. (Special mention may be made of the World Council of Churches, the British Council of Churches, the World's Student Christian Federation; for particular officers or committees of these or other bodies; for theologians at work on the doctrine of the Church; etc.)

V. Lord, we believe in thee;
R. *Help thou our unbelief.*

For a renewed commitment to her mission; and for all those who serve that mission through prayer, by gifts, as ministers of the gospel, evangelists, teachers, doctors, nurses, administrators (here may be mentioned some who have gone to the service of the Church overseas, perhaps from this college, or those responsible for leadership in the missionary societies and the International Missionary Council, or for the work of the Overseas Committee; for those who are uncertain if their vocation is to the service of the Church overseas): *V.* and *R.*

For the Church under trial, where she is persecuted or hampered by the evil intentions of men, where she is frustrated by the indifference of her members or the hardness of men's hearts (make special mention of particular areas where the problems of the Church are known to you): *V.* and *R.*

Let us pray for all men:

for men without hope in this world or faith in any other;

for persecutors, the callous and indifferent;

for the broken in spirit;

for the homeless, the stateless and all wanderers;

for God's ancient people the Jews;

for adherents of other faiths;

for students from other countries at present studying in this country (college, university);

for men and women from this country, in the service of society, industry or government overseas;

for ourselves, and for all who cause others to stumble;
for a manifestation of the power of God to pardon, to convince and to heal: *V*. and *R*.

Let us pray: Part IV, No. 153, or the following short litany:

V. Lord, have mercy upon us;
R. *Christ, have mercy upon us.*
V. Lord, have mercy upon us;
R. *Our Father . . .*
V. Set up thyself, O God, above the heavens;
R. *And thy glory above all the earth.*
V. Give thy Son the heathen for his inheritance;
R. *And the utmost parts of the earth for his possession.*
V. Let all nations whom thou hast made;
R. *Come and worship thee, O Lord.*
V. Let thy Name be great among the heathen, O Lord of hosts;
R. *And in every place let incense be offered to thy Name, and a pure offering.*
V. The Lord's Name be praised;
R. *From the rising up of the sun unto the going down of the same.*

Let us pray: Part IV, No. 151.

Ascription of Glory: Part IV, No. 226 or from No. 230.

VOCATION AND CAREERS

This section is designed to assist the thinking and prayers of those who are concerned with fulfilling their vocation as they consider the careers open to students. The section is arranged in three divisions: 1. Meditations; 2. A form of self-examination; 3. Devotions for use in private or corporate prayer.

(1) Meditations

This section contains suggestions for the making of three meditations. The Scripture headings give a general title for each. A prayer should be used as a preparation. See Part IV. In each case nothing is said about the type of prayer and resolution which will arise from the meditation. These are left to be formed by the person who meditates.

1. *Ye have not chosen me, but I have chosen you.*

Scripture passage. Matt. 4. 18-22.

Consider that all our powers of mind and body are God's gifts to us;
that our thanksgiving is the use of these gifts in his service;
that these gifts enable us to obey him in a particular way through the career to which he calls us;

that this calling means for us hardship and adventure, many friends and many enemies.

2. *Beloved of God, called to be saints.*
Scripture passage. Matt. 4. 1-11.
Consider that our Lord's temptation was to do the right thing in the wrong way;
that our temptation is often to do the wrong thing;
that God leads us into the true way and sustains us in following it;
that he does not guide us against our will;
that he answers our strivings to know his will for us;
that our strivings begin in being receptive and are continued in our active obedience to the divine prompting;
that our security is that peace which the world cannot give;
that our peace is active obedience in the face of danger and difficulty.

3. *I made myself a servant unto all.*
Scripture passage. John 13. 1-11.
Consider the magnitude of our Lord's service;
that our service begins in realization of our responsibilities and powers;
that in the eyes of God our purpose determines the importance of our work—not its nature;
that service is the fulfilment of the obligations which are ours because of our relationships to God and to men;
that our service to our family, the community and

the nation is interpreted to us by our membership of the Church;
that the following of a career, under the guidance of God, is to be our way of expressing our obedience to him.

Bible passages for further meditations. Exod. 3. 1-14; Isa. 6. 1-8; Jer. 1. 4-10; Matt. 3. 13-17; 9. 35-38; 12. 46-50; 19. 16-22; 20. 17-23; Luke 5. 27-28.

(2) A Form of Self-Examination (For Private Use)

Thou requirest truth in the inward parts
And shalt make me to understand wisdom secretly.
My soul truly waiteth still upon God
For of him cometh my salvation.

I. Have I thought out fully enough
 the careers open to my choice?
 the type of service to God which each would entail for me?
 that work gives meaning to my membership of the Church and of society?

II. Have I always been grateful for
 my abilities, my distinctness as a person?
 the advice and encouragement of those whom I respect?
 the powers which I found were mine through taking my part in common activities?
 all the ways God guides me towards finding my work and my place in life?

III. Have I always been ready to admit the anxieties that are
caused by vague unexamined fears?
frustrations due to financial difficulties?
family misunderstandings?
commitments I have already made?
obligations not of my own making?

IV. Am I sometimes inclined
to postpone deliberations about my career because I doubt my abilities and my worth?
to day-dream about a possible importance for myself of my own choosing?
to long for safety rather than adventure?
to shrink from consideration of certain careers because of the responsibility and temptations which they appear to have for me?
to forget that a career is a way of serving God and growing in knowledge of him that this service may be more mature?
to think too briefly about the nature of missionary obligations and how they may concern me?
to ignore the diverse ways in which God reveals his will for me—through events, happenings, friendships, my thinking and my praying?

V. How can I improve my thinking and my praying so that I may come more fully under the divine guidance?
What practical information do I require to help me to arrive at a decision about my career?
Is the choice about a career to be binding, or in my case can I make a provisional choice?

Lord, what I have not, give me.
Lord, what I know not, teach me.
Lord, what I am not, make me.

Almighty God, whose ways are past wonder, whose desires for us are beyond imagining; grant us wisdom and daring, that, with thine aid, we may serve thee in all faithfulness so that we may attain at length thy gracious promises; through Jesus Christ our Lord.

(3) Devotions for Use in Private or Corporate Prayer

This section provides devotions suitable for either private or corporate prayer. It can of course be used as a whole or in part according to occasion and need. The section is divided into three parts: (i) praise and thanksgiving; (ii) confession of sins; (iii) intercessions.

(i)

Holy, Holy, Holy, is the Lord God, the almighty, which was and is and which is to come.
Worthy art thou, our Lord and our God, to receive the glory and the honour and the power; for thou didst create all things, and because of thy will they were, and were created.
V. O Lord, thy word endureth for ever in heaven;
R. Thy truth also remaineth from one generation to another.
Here may follow a hymn of praise.
Jesus said: "Your joy no man taketh from you."

Let us rejoice in our several powers of mind and body:
the gifts of sight and perception;
memory and understanding;
vision and imagination;
touch and skill;
intuition and reason;
determination and intelligence;
whereby we are able to fashion things according to our purposes; whereby we discover words, sounds, shapes, and actions to express our delights and our needs in speech, music and the arts.

V. Let us bless the Lord;
R. Thanks be to God.

Let us rejoice in the ways through which the grace of God illuminates our common life with meaning and joy:
for the dignity of being human;

*R. We thank thee, O God.**

for all through whom thou hast led us to appreciate wisdom, gaiety, strength and tenderness;
for all who have led us to find the richness of our own abilities;
for maturity which interprets and is interpreted by our work;
for membership of the body of Christ which seals all our diverse powers and relationships in the unity of adoration.

V. Direct me in the path thou biddest me to follow;
R. All my musings shall be of thy wonderful deeds.

Our Father . . .

* Throughout this section the response is to follow each phrase.

(ii)

Jesus said: "Thou shalt love the Lord thy God with all thy heart, with all thy mind and with all thy strength. This is the first and great commandment and the second is like unto it, thou shalt love thy neighbour as thyself."

Our work is meant to be an expression of our love of God and of our neighbour.

Let us remember in penitence:

the sins of men which cause all work to be in conflict with the loving purpose of God;

R. Lord, have mercy upon us.

our pride and fear which accentuate this conflict;

R. Good Lord, forgive.

our failure to realize the full demands of our work upon us;

our blindness to the needs of the people of our time which causes neglect of work both here and abroad;

our lack of courage to express in our actions what we believe to be true;

our self-righteous views about our own work;

our tendency to envy, ambition and desire for ease;

our anxiety and its outcome of practical atheism.

O God, our Father, forgive us for what we have been, sanctify what we are, and order what we shall be; through Jesus Christ our Lord.

(Here a space of silence should be observed. In the silence will be found an opportunity to ask God's blessing upon the practical ways in which we can make amendment according to his grace. This devotion should conclude with the Lord's Prayer.)

(iii)

Jesus said: "Think not that I am come to send peace on earth, I came not to send peace, but a sword."

Let us pray that the might of God may enlarge us and make us bold:

against all who cleverly mock at high intentions;

R. Strengthen us, Good Lord.

against all who discount any purity in motives;

against all who deny that there is any meaning in life;

against all who guide their lives by expediency;

against all who distort the good news of the Gospel;

against all who believe in the power of men apart from God;

against all who would urge us to look for narrow temporal security;

against all kindly people who would encourage us to lose our souls in exchange for illusory comforts.

Let us pray for deliverance from all that weakens faith in God:

from pompous solemnity;

R. Good Lord, deliver us.

from mistaking earnestness for trust in thee;

from seeking easy answers to large questions;

from being overawed by the self-confident;

from dependence upon mood and feelings;

from despondency and loss of self-respect;

from timidity and hesitation in making decisions.

Let us pray for:

all who halt, uncertain before alternatives;

R. Hear us, we beseech thee, O Lord.

all who fear the commonplace;
all who must forgo much to achieve little;
all ordination candidates, especially . . . ;
all others who are also preparing to serve God according to their several callings; especially . . . ;
all examining obligations to work abroad, especially . . .

III

A HOLY PEOPLE

PREPARATION FOR THE HOLY COMMUNION

In their different churches students will have been taught how to prepare themselves for Holy Communion. This preparation will always include private devotions, and other parts of this book contain material which could be used in that way.

Members of the Student Christian Movement ought to approach this feast having in mind their membership in Christ's Body as a world-wide fellowship in which men of different Christian traditions share. To recognize another man as "in Christ" is to recognize him as a fellow-member of Christ's Church. Almost all Christians would claim that in this sacrament they in a quite special way receive Christ and are kept in membership of his body. The sacraments of Baptism and the Lord's Supper, and the Bible, are the great common possessions of Christian people. In these sacraments we are most at one with Christ, and therefore most at one with one another.

Yet at the Lord's table it is most evident that we are divided. There is no place where men are so clearly sinners as the place where they receive the greatest grace. For theological and disciplinary reasons we often may not receive this sacrament together. The pain and sorrow of this sinful state ought to be felt acutely throughout the whole Christian family. To an interdenominational fellowship like the S.C.M. the scandal of our divisions is particularly evident: the obligation to make an act of penitence is therefore particularly strong.

S.C.M. members can do two things:
1. At conferences, on the Saturday night, at least part of the evening prayers of the conference can be directed towards the common preparation of ourselves as one family for receiving in our sinfully divided state the Holy Communion on the next morning.
2. In our private prayers and at every celebration of the sacrament we can give thanks to God for the reality of Christ's presence in those celebrations in which our fellows are taking part, but from which we are absent. And we can and must repent for our divided state, and intercede for the peace and unity of the Church. (This will also be our duty on those occasions when we attend a celebration of the Holy Communion in a tradition other than our own, whether or not we are communicating.)
The following readings and prayers are only suggestions. Parts of them may be used as a basis on which to construct a service of preparation, or for private meditation.

Readings: Psalms 84, 116; Mark 10. 32-45; John 17; I. Cor. 1. 1-18; 11. 17-34; 12. 12-31; Eph. 2. 11-22; 4. 1-16.

Thanksgivings

How amiable are thy tabernacles, O Lord of Hosts.

For the joy and refreshment of the Church's worship;
for the great family who day by day and week by week, down the ages, and throughout the world, have found their rest at God's altar.

He steadfastly set his face to go to Jerusalem.

For him who for the joy that was set before him endured the cross;
for the holy supper of his body and blood, instituted in the night on which he was betrayed;
for his humility in being present to feed us in this sacrament.

That they may all be one.

For Jew and Greek, bond and free, male and female who have found their unity through partaking of the one body of Christ;
for this my brother (my fellow-student, member of this conference, of this Movement) with whom I shall be at one in receiving this sacrament.

Penitence

Wherewithal shall I come?
The sacrifices of God are a broken spirit.

For failure to discern the Lord's Body:
by easy acceptance of its divisions;
by regarding as trivial differences of conviction about this holy sacrament;
by intolerance, and denial of the claim of others to have met Christ at his own table.

For fainting hearts and faithless lives:

by failure to believe in the power of Christ's prayer for the unity of his Church;

by timidity in making some new venture in understanding what is unfamiliar, or fellowship with those from whom we differ.

Intercessions

I in them and thou in me, that they may be perfected into one; that the world may know . . .

For the visible unity of the whole Church of God;
for the universal mission of the Church of God;
for my fellow-members of the Student Christian Movement, especially those from whom I am divided by denomination: that we may be one;
for myself as I prepare to receive this sacrament;
for us all: that we may look up into the face of our Saviour and live.

Bidding, which could be used as part of a service of preparation.

We come not to this supper as righteous in ourselves; we come to seek our life in Christ. This sacrament is a singular medicine for all poor sick creatures, a comfortable help to weak souls; and our Lord requires no other worthiness on our part but that we unfeignedly acknowledge our sin. Wherefore we confess our unrighteousness, beseeching God to forgive our division, to heal our schisms, and by this sacrament to unite us in the holy Christ and make us acceptable in him.

Suggested by John Knox's Exhortation

Prayers

Before receiving the Sacrament:

Almighty and everlasting God, behold we approach the sacrament of thy only-begotten Son, our Lord Jesus Christ. As sick, we come to the physician of life; as unclean, to the fountain of mercy; as blind, to the light of eternal splendour; as needy, to the Lord of heaven and earth; as naked, to the king of glory. We implore therefore the abundance of thine infinite majesty, that thou wouldest vouchsafe to heal our sickness, to wash our foulness, to enlighten our darkness, to enrich our poverty, and to clothe our nakedness, that we may receive the king of kings and lord of lords, with such reverence and fear, such contrition and love, such faith and purity, such devotion and humility, as is expedient for the welfare of our souls. Grant us, we beseech thee, to receive not only the sacrament of the Lord's body and blood, but also the substance and virtue of the sacrament. O most merciful God, grant us so to receive the body of thy only-begotten Son, our Lord Jesus Christ, that we may be incorporated in his mystical body, and ever reckoned among his members. And, O most loving Father, grant us that whom we purpose to receive under a veil, we may at length behold with open face, even thy beloved Son; who with thee and the Holy Ghost liveth and reigneth, ever one God, world without end.

St. Thomas Aquinas

After receiving the Sacrament:

Psalm 150.

The *Nunc Dimittis*.

O God, who feedest us thy children with the true manna, the living bread from heaven; grant, we beseech thee, that this precious food may be our support throughout our earthly pilgrimage, until we reach that land where is neither hunger nor thirst; through Jesus Christ, our Lord.

Priest's Book of Private Devotion

Strengthen, O Lord, the hands which have been stretched out to receive thy holy things, that they may daily bring forth fruit to thy divine glory. Grant that the ears which have heard thy songs may be closed to the voice of clamour and dispute; that the eyes which have seen thy great love may also uphold thy blessed hope; that the tongues which have uttered thy praise may speak the truth; that the feet which have walked in thy courts may walk in the region of light; that the souls and bodies which have fed upon thy living body may be restored to newness of life. And with us may thy great love for ever abide, that we may abundantly render back praise, praise to thy sovereignty.

The Liturgy of Malabar

MEDITATIONS ON THE LORD'S SUPPER

"As often as ye eat this bread and drink this cup, ye do shew the Lord's death till he come."

The Meaning of his Sacrifice

O Sovereign Lord, Creator of all things,
because thou art what thou art
  and I am only thy creature,
therefore should I offer *sacrifice* to thee.
No act or offering short of sacrifice
  can express my obligations and my duties
or thy rights over me.
No other act can be so rich in meaning
  none so much my own and so complete;
therefore sacrifice is due from me to thee.
It is the best, the highest act I can perform,
  and my whole nature, my full self is in it,
therefore it is reserved to thee alone.

Sacrifice is thine, my God, and thine exclusively
because it rises from my deepest self,
  pervades, affects me through and through,
involving all the substance of my soul
in absolute surrender unto thee.

To others I may give but parts
or fragments of my self—
words, deeds, affections, thoughts.
But only unto thee my total self, my all,
because thou alone art God.

But when I think
how good and wonderful are thy works,
O Lord God Almighty,
how just, how high, how holy,
are all thy ways,
how exalted thy nature, how infinite thy power,
and how I am but dust and ashes, frail and weak,
wayward also, and marred by sin,
I dare not hold up to heaven and offer to thee
so poor, so spoilt a thing as I.
Therefore I turn to that divine love
which opened wide its arms to me on Calvary,
and still holds them daily open in this holy sacrament
to thy beloved Son, my mediator, I turn,
to him who drew me and took me to himself upon the Cross
and made me his,
blending and mingling, as water with red wine,
my poor life with his own,
so that together we two are one,
To him I turn, in him I trust, with him I stand identified.
Look then upon him, and me in him,
and not on me apart.
See his worth, not my demerit,

see his goodness, not my sin,
see his perfection, not my deficiency,
and accept from me through him and with him the oblation of myself.

After Communion
The Fruit of the Tree of Life

Thou art, Lord Jesus, the tree of life,
thou art the mystic vine,
and I a branch and one with thee,
as branch and tree are one.
If only I might understand this unity,
and my need of thee and my dependence,
also thy presence in my soul,
which extends and spreads thy incarnate life
and continues it in me.
A branch apart can bear no fruit,
nor even keep itself alive.
It must be fed by the flow of sap continuously.
So is it, Lord, between thee and me.
Cut off from thee I can do no good,
practise no Christian virtue.
Thy spirit must run into and possess
all the channels and fibres of my life
to reinforce and sanctify my earthly nature.
Thy power must mingle with my poverty of soul
unceasingly as nutriment and vital sap,
that I may say with truth,
"Now not I live, but Christ lives in me."

I have learned, Lord Jesus, what thy life means,
and tasted of its ripest, sweetest fruit,

I have seen the pattern and example,
in Bethlehem, in Nazareth, and on the Cross,
of what thou wouldst produce in me.
How can I ever lead a life like thine!
How show such fruit of virtue
in childlike submission and self-sacrifice!
Thy example would leave me helpless, in despair,
if thou didst not give us day by day our daily bread—
thy strength, thy energy, thy fertile power.
O fill each faculty as full as it can hold of thee,
that virtue may not be a burden and a task
but as thy life-blood in my veins.
Then let me never by any crookedness or opposition
check the inflow of thy power.
Let me submit with docile obedience to the
pruning-knife of thy providence
and to the discipline of thy Church,
lest I dishonour or discredit
thy inward influence of grace, which subjects itself
so humbly to my needs,
and while it nourishes
would transform and change me, in some sort, into
thee,
that I may share eternity with thee.

Adapted from W. Roche

MEDITATION OR MENTAL PRAYER

Prayer is not just thinking pious thoughts; still less is it saying pious words. One of the most important parts of prayer is that part which is just direct, even if only momentary, converse with God. No Christian has begun to grow up in the prayer life until he or she becomes aware of this as the real "praying" element in prayer.

But to get to this point, and especially to be able to sustain it for more than a second or two, is not easy, and requires hard work—like everything else worth-while. How do we set about the hard work? It is the experience of the majority of serious Christians that the best way to start off is by "meditation" or (better called) "mental prayer": to spend, that is to say, a fixed time every day or every week with one's Bible, drawing upon some short passage or incident or even phrase, getting every possible truth out of it, building it into one's life. Some will find that they cannot concentrate for longer than ten minutes at a time upon one theme; but they will, with practice, come to spend that ten minutes more and more fruitfully. Others may be able to manage longer. Half an hour per day is the ideal, but not everybody can spare that time. We must just give what time we have got; God will make use of it.

There are at least five " classical " methods of meditation, but it will only confuse the beginner to give them all. Let us be content with two typical ones, which suit roughly the two types of mind into which most of mankind are divided up.

(*A*) *The " Ignatian " Method* (St. Ignatius of Loyola) This may seem complicated. When put into practice it is not so, since the " stages " pass easily into each other, and in any case (as we shall explain later) need not all be equally dwelt upon.

I. " Preliminary preparation ": viz., selecting the passage of Holy Scripture to be used, and, very generally, what in it we propose to emphasize. This is best done the night before. Commentaries, B.R.F. notes, etc., will be useful here.

II. When we come to the actual time of prayer, we start by a brief introduction: dedication of the time to God; faith, adoration, contrition.

III. The meditation proper:

(*a*) Recall the biblical subject chosen, and the points in it to be considered.

(*b*) Picture the scene: go there in person, make all as vivid as the imagination can contrive.

(*c*) Ask God to bring the scene home to us, to make it operate inside us, so to speak: to give us an inner knowledge of him.

IV. The body of the meditation, applying memory, understanding and will to the subject we are considering:

(*a*) Remember what we have been thinking about the subject: remember our past lives—e.g., our neglect of the truths we find in the passage, etc.

(*b*) Work with our intellects upon the real meaning of the passage—the saying of our Lord or of St. Paul, the incident in Christ's life, etc.

(*c*) Make acts of the will, determining to profit by the lessons here learned: "What does this passage imply, for my action to-day, this week, the rest of my life?" So we make a resolution; and conclude with brief converse with God—the heart uttering praise, petition, adoration, etc.

V. The conclusion. Gathering up the fruits of the meditation, examining our own conduct of it—our perseverance at it, our concentration, our distractions, etc. Prayer to pray better next time.

Let us briefly take an example. Say we have chosen the scene of our Lord by the lake-side and the miraculous draught of fishes (John 21). Then when we come to section III, we shall think of the passage, which we read over the night before; try to picture it clearly—walk by the lake ourselves, or sit in the boat with the disciples. Then, under IV we shall (*a*) remember all we can about our Lord's power and our own weakness.

This will naturally lead on to

(*b*) the work of our minds on the passage (a Biblical commentary may have helped us when we read it through first; now we can use what it tells us, e.g. about parallel passages in the gospels, the meaning of the original words, the symbolism employed, e.g. in " Cast the net *on the right side* of the boat, and ye shall find ").

(*c*) But so far this is a bit external and academic. Now we must pray the passage: apply it to ourselves, and make acts of the will in connection with it (e.g. We are despondent sometimes because we find so little result—in ourselves or in others—for our spiritual labours. But he is always there, if only we will trust him. So often we do not recognize him—we need a miracle before we will say, " It is the Lord." Let us resolve to keep our eyes skinned for him in future; to have more faith in his power, more obedience . . . etc.)

The elaborateness of this method is really to help those who find it hard to concentrate for long: it gives them plenty to do, plenty of movement from one consideration to another. But some will find the system holding them up—and even those who start with this method may later find they want to move on to another more flexible.

The best method to move on to then is probably:

(B) The " Sulpician " method

The preparation is as in I and II above.

The meditation proper consists in three simple acts:

(*a*) Jesus before the eyes (adoration). Out of the passage selected we pick merely the attribute of our Lord there exhibited (his power, or his compassion, his sternness with evil, his understanding and tact . . . etc.).

(*b*) Jesus in the heart (communion). Here he comes, with those attributes we have just adored in him, to pass them on to us, to pour them into our hearts. This will show up our own poverty, and in our thankfulness we shall be very humble and contrite for our unworthiness.

(*c*) Jesus in the hands (co-operation). We must not be content with pious thoughts about him and pleasant feelings: by their fruits they will be known. Resolution to work with and for him, to let him work in us.

This second method is very simple, and may lead those who use it to pass in the end beyond " meditation " (which is so much the work of the intellect) to even simpler kinds of praying, with the heart and affections—to prayer which consists in merely looking at our Lord, saying and thinking nothing; in contemplation of him while we repeat short phrases, even single words, over and over again; in just being quiet, not consciously making any effort to think or pray, but vaguely aware that he envelops and surrounds and upholds us all the time. This is not the place to describe this kind of prayer. It comes to many; if it comes it must not be evaded; but it will not come to any who will not work for it, who will not put aside time for prayer. It is not, therefore, a substitute for those who do not like the donkey-work; and it certainly comes only to those who are really convinced that praying is the most practical and the most important activity of all. In any case, whatever the kind of prayer we are called to, one fundamental maxim applies to all; prayer being a personal relationship, the work of the intellect can only be preparatory to the real thing—converse with God.

SELF-EXAMINATION

No one can make your self-examination except yourself. That stands to reason. The hints given below are not meant to do it for you. They are only suggestions to start you off on your own—like thawing a frozen pipe. It is best to tackle the job positively. Lists of " sins " are too like a school marking sheet. We run through them and say, " Good: only six out of a hundred." But if we look at what God wants of us, we shan't let ourselves off so lightly.

Normally the Beatitudes; or the Ten Commandments; or the two headings, " My duty to God ", " to my neighbour ", are a good way to start. Every day, or at least every week, a quick glance at them, and then at ourselves in the light of them, will do.

But from time to time we need to be more searching. Perhaps before some major decision or event in our lives; or once a year when we can get some quiet time. Then the following considerations may help. But they are not to be used regularly, daily or anything like that. They may sometimes be used before going to receive Holy Communion. It may be better to concentrate thoroughly upon one or two points, rather than a hurried run through the whole list.

We might start quite low down in the scale, with the

" righteousness " of scribes and pharisees (Matt. 5. 20). Even non-Christians try to live by these:

(1) *Justice*, or *Righteousness*. (Psalms 15; 119. 7.) Am I careful about my dealings with others? About a fair deal for those who cannot defend themselves—especially if I do not care for them? About the practices (financial, political, etc.) of those on whom I directly depend? About the standards adopted by those with whom I am identified and whom I am afraid to rebuke?
Righteousness means a care for truth. Am I careful what I say publicly about the characters of others? Or what I think privately about the same without troubling to investigate the truth? Do I let others make incorrect statements which I know I could (and should) challenge?
Do I tell lies to give a good impression of myself? (Did I pretend to have read a book, when in reality I had only read a review of the book?) Do my views change according to the company I happen to be in? Am I afraid of the truth, lest it disturb my faith?

(2) *Temperance*, or *self-control*. (I Cor. 9. 27.) My body is the temple of the Holy Ghost. Is it fit for him to dwell in? Do I keep my temper in rein? My affections? Do I squander my talents, instead of using them for God? Am I disciplined in my work? In my leisure? In my spending? Do my self-indulgences (smoking, " flicks ", drink, food, lazing about) hinder my effectiveness in his service? Do I use the company

of others (young men, young women) merely for my own pleasures and sensations? Am I slack about dress, cleanliness, getting up in the morning, going to bed in good time? Have I developed bad habits which are irritating or hurtful to others; demoralizing to myself? Do I use my time well? How much in gossip? How much in prayer?

(3) *Fortitude.* (Eph. 6. 10.) Christian fortitude is more than natural courage. Do I persevere when I don't seem to be making headway? Am I afraid of public opinion? Do I exaggerate my naturalness for fear of being thought pious? Can I stand up to the scorn of the clever? Am I afraid to put myself to learn, especially from simple people of deeper spiritual maturity than I? Am I really willing to embark on the Christian journey, wherever it may land me? Am I afraid of my own lack of fortitude?

(4) *Prudence*, or *Wisdom*. (Luke 16. 8.) There is a selfish, calculating prudence. But there is also a right kind of prudence, which keeps the various elements in our make-up in healthy proportion, and assesses situations wisely and far-sightedly.

Do I allow one part of me to dominate unduly over the rest? Am I obtrusively "intellectual"? Or "physical"? Too hearty with those who might resent it? Tactless? Do I pretend to be solemn and "religious"? Is my scrupulosity really criticism, a fault-finding attitude to others? Do I develop my sense of humour? Do I swamp people with over-emotionalism? Do I excuse myself from responsibility by saying that "politics is a dirty business"? Do I know "my station in life and its duties"?

These four are "natural" virtues. But more is demanded of Christians. "If ye do good to them that do good to you what thank have ye? for even sinners do the same" (Luke 6. 33).

We are also called to

(1) *Faith.* (Matt. 7. 20.) Not merely assent with the mind, but faith *in* a person. Do I believe that God can work miracles with me? (Do I want him to?) Or with others (even those of whom we say, "Oh, they're quite impossible")? Do I believe that God can forgive? That he can conquer my bad habits? Do I seek forgiveness only to soothe my feelings, without intending to give up the sins I want forgiven? Is my faith strong enough for me to launch out into the deep? Or do I rely half on faith, half on one foot still touching the ground? Have I faith in the hidden goodness of evil characters? In God's power to prevail even through the dissensions of Christians; through the intellectual problems of philosophy, science, psychology, etc.; through power politics; through the stupidity of the well-intentioned? Do I believe in the power of prayer? Is my worship of God merely conventional, or vital with living faith?

(2) *Hope.* (Rom. 8. 24; Col. 1. 27.) A "desperate hope" is a contradiction in terms: either we hope or we don't. Christian hope is based on the promises of God. Do I look for the blessed hope and appearing

in glory of our great God, and saviour Jesus Christ? (Tit. 2. 13.) Does my hope in God show itself by my bearing, my outlook on life? Do I know the meaning of Christian joy? Do I excuse myself for a moping and demoralizing gloom by saying I believe in "original sin"? Am I morbidly introspective? Do I take a delight in finding my worst prognostications vindicated? Do I encourage hope in others?

(3) *Charity*, "*Love*". (I Cor. 13.) Not just natural "kindliness", but the love of God shed abroad in our hearts through the Holy Ghost which is given to us. (Rom. 5. 5.) So it starts from our relations with God, and then passes to our relations with our neighbour. When I talk about "loving God" am I merely using a trite phrase? Do I try to get to know him better—by prayer? by study? through the lives of great Christians who have loved him? through better worship and obedience? Do I constantly see his will as the axle of the universe? Do I detect the goodness of all things else as valuable only in him?
Does my love of God show itself in gratitude? In constant praise? In willingness to give—not merely "what I can spare", but all? In glad acceptance of pain, tedium, costing effort, disappointment, disillusion, sorrow? Do I look only for nice feelings, fervent experiences, in prayer? Am I willing to put up with the difficulties, the dry patches, of the spiritual life? Do I want things too easy? Have I dictated to God in prayer? Have I shown my love for him by keeping his commands—about Sunday worship; about

marriage; about respect for life and others' goods; etc.? Do I suffer from self-pity?
Do I try to love others for what God sees good in them? Am I ready to forgive and go on forgiving? Do I pray regularly and *sympathetically* for my enemies? Am I grateful for criticism of myself? Am I glad when others go wrong? Am I generous in service of others? In alms? Do I get tired of trying to love people? Am I jealous of others' goods? talents? superiority over me? good looks? spiritual progress? Do I try to love the unattractive? Those who get on my nerves? The stupid? The inefficient? Have I acted charitably with the thought that others' gratitude might come in useful one day; or that I might gain credit with the world for it; or that I might be remembered in a will? Have I curried favour with the great and influential? Shown kindness only to toadies who would sing my praises, whom I could boss around? Have I loved sufficiently to be stern where necessary, even if it made me criticized? Have I taken things for granted—from my parents; from past benefactors; from institutions; from society; from God? Have I taken the trouble to put myself in others' shoes? Have I condoned uncharity in others? Or even joined in it? Do I always manage to get to the front of the queue? To get a seat in crowded trains? Do I respect others' opinions? Do I think of the example I set to those whom I influence? Do I consult those who would be hurt not to be consulted, even if I know their advice may be of little use? Am I patient with the irritable; the slow-witted; the

ungrateful? Do I rejoice in the Lord and all his creatures? Do I rejoice, and again I say, rejoice?

Then say Psalm 51. And perhaps a prayer from Part IV, Nos. 79-112.

Note. If you are still not satisfied with the suggestions given above you may find further help in:

D. Sayers, *The Other Six Deadly Sins*. (Methuen).

A. Wilson, *Pardon and Peace*, chap. viii. (Sheed & Ward).

M. Jarrett-Kerr, C.R., *Our Trespasses*, chap. iv. (S.C.M. Press).

IV

A TREASURY OF CHRISTIAN PRAYER

INVOCATION AND CALL TO WORSHIP

From the Bible

Psalm 65. 2	Hab. 2. 20
90. 1 and 2	Matt. 11. 28-30
95. 1 and 2 (or to 7)	John 4. 23-24
96. 9 (or to 13)	I Cor. 3. 16
99. 1 (B.C.P.)	Phil. 4. 4-7
Isa. 40. 31	Heb. 10. 19-22a
55. 6 (or to 7)	12. 1-2
57. 15	I John 4. 16b

(1) In the name of the Father and of the Son and of the Holy Spirit. Grace and peace be to you from God our Father and our Lord Jesus Christ.

(2) O Lord our God, great, eternal, wonderful in glory, who keepest covenant and promise for those that love thee with their whole heart, who art the life of all, the help of those that flee unto thee, the hope of those who cry unto thee; cleanse us from our sins, and from every thought displeasing to thy goodness, that with a pure heart and a clean mind, with perfect love and calm hope, we may venture confidently and fearlessly to pray unto thee, through Jesus Christ our Lord.

Coptic Liturgy of St. Basil (4th Century)

(3) O come, let us worship God our king. O come, let us worship and fall down before Christ, our king and our God.
O come, let us worship and fall down before the very Christ our king and our God. O come, let us worship and fall down before him.

The Liturgy of St. John Chrysostom (4th Century)

(4) O God, who art life and truth and blessedness, the only good, our hope and our heart's joy; we thank thee that thou hast created us in thine image, and that we can direct our thoughts to thee. Make us to know thee aright, and to enjoy and possess thee more and more; through Jesus Christ our Lord.

St. Anselm (12th Century)

(5) O Lord, open thou our lips;
And our mouth shall shew forth thy praise.
O God, make speed to save us;
O Lord, make haste to help us.
Glory be to the Father, and to the Son, and to the Holy Ghost;
As it was in the beginning, is now and ever shall be: world without end.

Book of Common Prayer

(6) Almighty God, unto whom all hearts be open, all desires known, and from whom no secrets are hid: cleanse the thoughts of our hearts by the inspiration of thy Holy Spirit, that we may perfectly love thee,

and worthily magnify thy holy name; through Christ our Lord.

Book of Common Prayer

(7) O God, who in thy love hast bestowed upon us gifts such as our fathers never knew nor dreamed of: mercifully grant that we be not so occupied with material things that we forget the things which are spiritual; lest, having gained the whole world, we lose our own soul; for thy mercy's sake.

G. W. Briggs (20th Century)

(8) O thou eternal Wisdom, whom we partly know and partly do not know; O thou eternal Justice, whom we partly acknowledge, but never wholly obey; O thou eternal Love, whom we love a little, but fear to love too much:

Open our minds, that we may understand;
Work in our wills, that we may obey;
Kindle our hearts, that we may love thee.
(Silence)
Amen, come Lord Jesus.

Source unknown

(9) Lord, I believe in thee, help thou mine unbelief; I love thee, yet not with a perfect heart as I would; I long for thee, yet not with my full strength; I trust in thee, yet not with my whole mind. Accept my faith, my love, my longing to know and serve thee, my trust in thy power to keep me. What is cold do thou kindle, what is lacking do thou make up. I wait thy blessing; through Jesus Christ our Lord.

Malcolm Spencer (20th Century)

ADORATION

From the Bible

Psalm 8
67
100
148
150
A large number of other passages can be found in the Psalms
Isa. 6. 3
40. selections from 12-end

Dan. 2. 20-22
Hab. 3. 17-18
Ecclus. 1. 2-3
Rom. 11. 33 (or to 36)
Eph. 3. 20-21
Rev. 4. 8-11
5. 12
7. 12
19. 5-6

(10) Glory be to the Father, and to the Son, and to the Holy Ghost: as it was in the beginning, is now, and ever shall be, world without end.

(11) Almighty God, whose glory the heavens are telling, the earth thy power, and the sea thy might, and whose greatness all feeling and thinking creatures everywhere proclaim; to thee belongeth glory, honour, might, greatness and magnificence now and for ever, and unto ages of ages, through Jesus Christ our Lord.

The Liturgy of St. James (4th Century)

(12) Worthy of praise from every mouth,
of confession from every tongue,
of worship from every creature,
is thy glorious name, O Father, Son and Holy Ghost:
who didst create the world in thy grace
and by thy compassion didst save the world.
To thy majesty, O God, ten thousand times ten thousand bow down and adore,
singing and praising without ceasing, and saying
Holy, holy, holy, Lord God of hosts;
heaven and earth are full of thy praises;
hosanna in the highest.

Nestorian Liturgy (*shortened*)

(13) Blessed be God for his incarnation.
Thou little Son of God, laid in a manger, we adore thee for thy coming! Now God is of our image, God is of our flesh and blood! Now is there no difference at all between thy flesh and ours! Thou art our saviour and our brother who liest in a crib! Thou liest in our misery, sharest our needs, assurest us of our glory. Halleluia!

Wilton Rix (*after M. Luther, 16th Century*)

(14) O God the Father of heaven,
who hast marvellously created the world out of nothing,
who dost govern and uphold heaven and earth with thy power,
who didst deliver thine only begotten for us unto death:

O God the Son, redeemer of the world,
who didst will to be incarnate of a virgin,
who hast washed us from our sins by thy precious blood,
who rising from the dead didst ascend victorious to heaven:
O God the Holy Ghost, the comforter,
who didst descend upon Jesus in the form of a dove,
who coming upon the apostles didst appear in fiery tongues,
who dost visit and confirm with thy grace the hearts of the saints:
O sacred, highest, eternal, blissful, blessed Trinity,
always to be praised, yet always unspeakable:
O Father good,
O Son loving,
O Spirit kind,

whose { majesty is unspeakable, power is incomparable, goodness is inestimable;

whose { work is life, love is grace, contemplation is glory:

Deity, Divinity, Unity, Trinity:
Thee I worship, thee I call upon,
with the whole affection of my heart I bless thee now and for ever more.

Preces Privatae, Lancelot Andrewes
(17th Century)

(15) Great, O Lord, is thy kingdom, thy power and thy glory; great are thy works, thy wonders and thy praises; great also is thy wisdom, thy goodness, thy justice, thy mercy; and for all these we do bless thee, and will magnify thy holy name for ever and ever.

George Wither (17th Century)

(16) Look up, my soul, and see the innumerable multitude of triumphing spirits.
Behold, the glorious angels fall down before the throne, and prostrate adore him that liveth for ever.
Hark how they fill that spacious temple with their hymns, while night and day they continually sing:
"Holy, holy, holy, Lord God of hosts!
Heaven and earth are full of thy glory—
Hallelujah."
Behold, the blessed saints lay their crowns at his feet, and on their faces adore him that liveth for ever and ever.
Nor is envy in them if we aspire to sing the same bright name which they adore;
Since there is but one family of us both in heaven and earth, under one head, and all are knit together by one Spirit.

John Austin (17th Century)

(17) Rejoice in God, O ye tongues: give the glory to the Lord and the Lamb.
Nations and languages and every creature, in which is the breath of life,

Let man and beast appear before him, and magnify his name together.

Christopher Smart (18th Century)

(18) Almighty God, most blessed and most holy, before the brightness of whose presence the angels veil their faces; with lowly reverence and adoring love we acknowledge thine infinite glory, and worship thee, Father, Son, and Holy Spirit, eternal Trinity. Blessing, and honour, and glory, and power be unto our God, for ever and ever.

Book of Common Order

(19) Holy art thou, O God the Father, who hast made of one blood all nations of the earth.
Holy art thou, O God the Son, who hast redeemed all mankind from the power of darkness.
Holy art thou, O God the Holy Spirit, giver of life and light, by whom the whole Church is governed and sanctified.
Holy art thou, O God the eternal and adorable Trinity, for whose glory man and all created things are, and were created.

Prayers of the World-Wide Church (S.P.G.)

CONFESSION AND PRAYERS FOR FORGIVENESS

FROM THE BIBLE

Psalm 51. 1-3 (or selection of verses from the whole psalm)
103. 8-13
139. 23-24
143. 2
Isa. 6. 5
Dan. 9. 9-10
Mic. 6. 8
Ecclus. 2. 17-18
Matt. 6. 14-15
7. 1-3
Luke 15. 18-19
18. 13-14
Rom. 6. 23
Heb. 4. 12-13
I John 1. 7-9

(20) Lord, for thy tender mercies' sake, lay not our sins to our charge, but forgive that is past and give us grace to amend our lives; to decline from sin and incline to virtue, that we may walk with a perfect heart before thee, now and evermore.

Ridley's Prayers, 1566

(21) Almighty and most merciful Father, We have erred and strayed from thy ways like lost sheep, We have followed too much the devices and desires of our own hearts, We have offended against thy holy laws, We have left undone those things which we ought to have done, And we have done those things which we

ought not to have done, And there is no health in us: But thou, O Lord, have mercy upon us, miserable offenders; spare thou them, O God, which confess their faults, Restore thou them that are penitent, According to thy promises declared unto mankind in Christ Jesu our Lord: And grant, O most merciful Father, for his sake, That we may hereafter live a godly, righteous and sober life, To the glory of thy holy name.

The General Confession, 1552 (Book of Common Prayer)

(22) *V.* O Saviour of the world, who by thy cross and precious blood hast redeemed us;

R. Save us and help us, we humbly beseech thee, O Lord.

Book of Common Prayer

(23) We confess to God almighty, the Father, the Son and the Holy Ghost, that we have sinned in thought, word and deed, through our own grievous fault. Wherefore we pray God to have mercy upon us.

Book of Common Prayer (1928)

(24) Forgive me my sins, O Lord, forgive me the sins of my youth and the sins of mine age, the sins of my soul, and the sins of my body, my secret and my whispering sins, my presumptuous and my crying sins, the sins that I have done to please myself, and the sins that I have done to please others. Forgive me those sins which I know, and those sins which I know

not; forgive them, O Lord, forgive them all, of thy great goodness.

Bishop Cosin (17th Century)

(25) Almighty and most merciful God, we acknowledge and confess that we have sinned against thee in thought, and word and deed; that we have not loved thee with all our heart and soul, with all our mind and strength; and that we have not loved our neighbour as ourselves. We beseech thee, O God, to be forgiving to what we have been, to help us to amend what we are, and of thy mercy to direct what we shall be, so that the love of goodness may ever be first in our hearts and we may follow unto our life's end in the steps of Jesus Christ our Lord.

John Hunter (20th Century)

(26) O God, who art never deceived: dispel the blindness of our heart; and so quicken our conscience that we may see ourselves as thou seest us; for Jesus Christ's sake.

G. W. Briggs

(27) Almighty and most merciful Father, we confess that we have sinned against thy love and against thy truth. Neither with heart, nor soul, nor strength, have we loved our neighbour as ourselves. We confess especially that we have not loved thee with our minds. We have not owned thy lordship in our thinking. Grant us, most merciful Father, pardon, absolution and remission of this and all our sin, and give us grace to love thee as we ought, through Jesus Christ our Lord.

(28) O thou giver of wisdom and skill, we confess that we have scorned those who labour mainly with their hands; we have prided ourselves upon our superior intellect, and have looked down upon the skilled hands and the honest labour of those who also maintain the fabric of the world, and in whose handicraft is their prayer. Take from us all that makes us unworthy of our privileges, and help us to remember that we are able to pursue our studies only because others perform their labours, through Jesus Christ our Lord.

(29) O God, by whose unchanging law the harvest follows the seed-time, and whatsoever is sown is afterward reaped: mercifully grant that we sow not such seed, that we and they who follow after us reap misery and shame; for Jesus Christ's sake.

G. W. Briggs

(30) O God, mercifully grant unto us that the fire of thy love may burn in us all things that displease thee, and make us meet for thy heavenly kingdom; for the sake of Jesus Christ our Saviour.

Roman Breviary (11th Century)

(31) O God, whose nature and property is ever to have mercy and to forgive, receive our humble petitions; and though we be tied and bound with the chain of our sins, yet let the pitifulness of thy great mercy loose us; for the honour of Jesus Christ, our mediator and advocate.

Book of Common Prayer

(32) May the almighty and merciful Lord grant unto you (*us*) pardon and remission of all your (*our*) sins, time for amendment of life, and the grace and comfort of the Holy Spirit.

Book of Common Prayer (1928)

(33) O Lamb of God,
that takest away the sins of the world,
Have mercy on us.
Thou that takest away the sins of the world,
Have mercy on us.
Thou that takest away the sins of the world,
Receive our prayer.
Thou that sittest at the right hand of God the Father,
Have mercy on us.

From Gloria in Excelsis

X (34) Almighty and everlasting God, who art always more ready to hear than we to pray, and art wont to give more than either we desire, or deserve: pour down upon us the abundance of thy mercy; forgiving us those things whereof our conscience is afraid, and giving us those good things which we are not worthy to ask, but through the merits and mediation of Jesus Christ, thy Son, our Lord.

Book of Common Prayer

(35) Grant, we beseech thee, merciful Lord, to thy faithful people pardon and peace, that they may be cleansed from all their sins, and serve thee with a quiet mind; through Jesus Christ our Lord.

Book of Common Prayer

(36) O Lord God, who shewest anger only with a view to mercy, and who threatenest in order to spare; stretch forth thy hand to the fallen, and in thy manifold pity give help to the struggling: that those whom thou hast redeemed may be kept by thine aid in the glorious hope of life everlasting, through Jesus Christ our Lord.

Gelasian Sacramentary

X (37) O God our Father, from whom all fatherhood in heaven and earth is named, graciously behold this thy family. Thou art ever merciful and makest thy sun to rise on the just and on the unjust. But we have misused thy gifts, marred thy work, and robbed one another of our daily bread. Help us to see and feel our share in the guilt of the world and grant us thy grace to bring forth fruits worthy of repentance, through Jesus Christ our Lord.

The Kingdom, the Power and the Glory

THANKSGIVING

From the Bible

Exod. 15. 2
I Chron. 29. 11-13
Psalm 50. 14
103. 1-4
136. 1-9
Wis. 11. 21-26
Matt. 11. 25-26
Rom. 8. 31-end
II Cor. 1. 3-4
Eph. 1. 3
I Pet. 1. 3-4
Rev. 15. 3b

(38) Almighty God, whose works are great beyond our understanding, and thou greater than all thy works: look in mercy upon us, as we endeavour to praise thee, whom no man is able worthily to praise; for thy loving kindness' sake.

From Ecclesiasticus

(39) Thou, O Lord, art mighty for ever. Thou causest the wind to blow and the rain to fall. Thou sustainest the living, quickenest the dead, supportest the falling, dost loose them that are bound, and keepest thy faith to them that sleep in the dust. Who is like unto thee, O Lord of mighty acts?

From the daily Jewish liturgy in our Lord's own day

(40) We give thanks to thee, O Lord God, Father almighty, together with thy Son our Lord and Saviour Jesus Christ, and the Holy Spirit. All nations offer praise and thanksgiving unto thee, O Lord, from the rising of the sun unto the going down thereof, from the north and from the south, for great is thy name in all nations.

Prayers of the World-Wide Church (adapted from the Liturgy of St. Mark)

(41) Glory be to God on high, and in earth peace, good will towards men. We praise thee, we bless thee, we worship thee, we glorify thee, we give thanks to thee for thy great glory, O Lord God, heavenly king, God the Father almighty.
O Lord, the only-begotten Son Jesu Christ; O Lord God, Lamb of God, Son of the Father, that takest away the sins of the world, have mercy upon us. Thou that takest away the sins of the world, have mercy upon us. Thou that takest away the sins of the world, receive our prayer. Thou that sittest at the right hand of God the Father, have mercy upon us. For thou only art holy; thou only art the Lord; thou only, O Christ, with the Holy Ghost, art most high in the glory of God the Father.

Fourth Century (Book of Common Prayer version)

(42) O most high, almighty, good Lord God, to thee belong praise, glory, honour and blessing!
Praised be my Lord God with all his creatures, and

especially our brother the sun, who brings us the day and who brings us the light; fair is he and shines with a very great splendour; O Lord, he signifies to us thee.
Praised be my Lord for our sister the moon, and for the stars, the which he has set clear and lovely in heaven.
Praised be my Lord for our brother the wind, and for air and cloud, calms and all weather, by the which thou upholdest life in all creatures.
Praised be my Lord for our sister water, who is very serviceable unto us and humble and precious and clean.
Praised be my Lord for our brother fire, through whom thou givest us light in the darkness; and he is bright and pleasant and very mighty and strong.
Praised be my Lord for our mother the earth, the which doth sustain us and keep us, and bringeth forth divers fruits, and flowers of many colours, and grass.
Praised be my Lord for all those who pardon one another for his love's sake, and who endure weakness and tribulation; blessed are they who peaceably shall endure, for thou, O most Highest, shalt give them a crown.
Praised be my Lord for our sister the death of the body, from which no man escapeth. Woe to him who dieth in mortal sin!
Blessed are they who are found walking by thy most holy will, for death shall have no power to harm them.
Praise ye and bless ye the Lord, and give thanks unto him, and serve him with great humility.

Thanksgiving of St. Francis

(43) Almighty God, Father of all mercies, We thine unworthy servants do give thee most humble and hearty thanks for all thy goodness and loving kindness to us, and to all men; We bless thee for our creation, preservation, and all the blessings of this life; but above all, for thine inestimable love in the redemption of the world by our Lord Jesus Christ; for the means of grace and for the hope of glory. And we beseech thee, give us that due sense of all thy mercies, that our hearts may be unfeignedly thankful, and that we shew forth thy praise, not only with our lips, but in our lives; by giving up ourselves to thy service, and by walking before thee in holiness and righteousness all our days; through Jesus Christ our Lord, to whom with thee and the Holy Ghost be all honour and glory, world without end.

General Thanksgiving 1552 (Book of Common Prayer)

(44) O God, most glorious, most bountiful, accept we humbly beseech thee, our praises and thanksgivings for thy holy catholic Church, the mother of us all who bear the name of Christ; for the faith which it hath conveyed in safety to our time, and the mercies by which it hath enlarged and comforted the souls of men; for the virtues which it hath established upon earth, and the holy lives by which it glorifieth both the world and thee; to whom, O blessed Trinity, be ascribed all honour, might, majesty, and dominion, now and for ever.

Memorials on Several Occasions

(45) O God of the spirits of all flesh; we praise and magnify thy holy name for thy saints and martyrs of every age, for the whole multitude of the redeemed, and for all thy servants dear to us, who, having finished their course, have entered into the joy of thy heavenly presence . . . ; and we beseech thee that we, being encouraged by their example and strengthened by their fellowship, may in the end have part with them in the inheritance of the saints in light; through the merits of thy Son, Jesus Christ our Lord.

Book of Common Order

(46) O God, we thank thee that thou hast called us into the fellowship of thy world-wide Church. Unite us, and all its members everywhere, in love and loyalty to carry out thy purpose of love in the world to-day. Grant that we may not fail thee in this day of opportunity; through Jesus Christ our Lord.

World-Wide Prayers in War-time

(47) O Saviour Jesus Christ, who, on the night before thy passion, didst pray that all may be made one, we praise and thank thee for the witness of the W.S.C.F. in past years; for its achievement in drawing together students of all nations in tolerance and understanding; for its care for the wholeness of mankind; for its rôle in the increasing unity of the Church; for the wisdom of its officers, and the generosity of its friends. We praise thee for the new opportunities thou art ever revealing to us in our generation; for the possibilities which challenge our obedience and test our faith. For

these and all thy mercies we bless thee, who with the Father and the Holy Spirit livest and reignest unto ages of ages.

(48) Lord, for the erring thought,
Not into action wrought;
Lord, for the wicked will,
Betrayed and baffled still;
For the heart from itself kept
Our thankfulness accept.

Book of Prayers for Students

(49) *An Act of Praise for the Creation*

Blessed art thou who didst create the dry land and the seas, and all the wonders that in them are.

And God called the dry land earth, and the gathering together of the waters called he seas . . . and God saw that it was good.

Instead of the deep were lakes and rivers and fountains;

Instead of the waste were islands, valleys and meadows;

Instead of the void were grass and trees and woodlands.

Praise be unto thee for the expanses of the continents;

For the calling forth of all the tribes of the earth from their cradle;

For the fertility of the earth;

For the secrets of fire, iron and corn thou didst reveal to men in primeval days;

For the marvels of radiation and space, and the inward nature of the atom revealed to him in these last days.

That the universe with unchanging fidelity varies its harmonious seasons, seeds of things discordant mutually keep an abiding covenant . . . that the greedy sea compels its waves to keep fixed limits, lest they should take the liberty of ever shifting the far-extended boundaries of the land. The Binder of this order of things, who rules the earth and sea, and holds sway in the very heavens, is LOVE. Should he let go the reins, all things that now live in mutual affection would be at continual strife, and would seek to break up the great machine, of which, with all its lovely motions, they are actually driving-forces. He it is who imposes on peoples the holy treaty of peace: who welds with chaste love the sacred bond of marriage: who promulgates his law to faithful comrades. O happy race of men, if Love, by whom the heavens are ruled, should also rule your souls.

W. Rix, Private and Public Prayers
(from Boethius)

(50) *Thanksgiving for the progress of the Gospel*

Thou art worthy, O Lord, to receive power,
And riches, and wisdom, and strength,
And honour, and glory, and blessing.
Blessed be thy glorious name
That thy word has sounded forth,
Not only in Jerusalem, and Antioch,
In Athens and in Rome;
But in every place the faith of Christ
Is spread abroad.
All glory be to thee.

For thy good soldiers in every age,
Striving lawfully, enduring unto the end,
  For wisdom of doctors,
  The zeal of evangelists,
  The eloquence of prophets,
  The love of pastors,
For the praises of babes, the ministry of women,
The purity of the young, the fervour of the aged,
  For all the signs of thy presence,
  All the marks of thy cross,
    All glory be to thee.
For the light of thy everlasting gospel,
Sent to every nation, and kindred, and tongue, and people,
  Shining so long amongst ourselves;
  For thy Church, the pillar and ground of the truth,
Against which the gates of hell have not prevailed.
  For thy gracious word of promise,
  That they that be wise shall shine
  As the brightness of the firmament,
And they that turn many to righteousness
  As the stars for ever and ever,
    All glory be to thee.
  The Lord is gracious and merciful,
  Long-suffering and of great goodness.
  The Lord is loving unto every man,
  And his mercy is over all his works.
  All thy works praise thee, O Lord,
  And thy saints give thanks unto thee.

They shew the glory of thy kingdom,
And talk of thy power.
That thy power, thy glory, and the mightiness of thy kingdom,
Might be known unto men;
Thy kingdom is an everlasting kingdom,
And thy dominion endureth throughout all ages.
Great and marvellous are thy works,
Lord God almighty,
Just and true are thy ways,
Thou King of saints.
Who shall not fear thee, O Lord, and glorify thy name?
For thou only art holy;
For all nations shall come and worship before thee;
For thy judgments are made manifest.
All glory be to thee.
After this I beheld, and, lo a great multitude,
Which no man could number,
Of all nations, and kindreds, and people, and tongues,
Stood before the throne and before the Lamb,
Clothed with white robes,
And palms in their hands;
And cried with a loud voice, saying,
Salvation to our God, which sitteth upon the throne,
And unto the Lamb.
Alleluia!
For the Lord God omnipotent reigneth.

Glory be to the Father, and to the Son, and to the Holy Ghost;
As it was in the beginning, is now, and ever shall be, world without end.

A Simple Form of Compline

PETITION

From the Bible

Psalm 57. 1-2
90. 12-end
119 (many verses e.g. 17-18)
Isa. 65. 24
Wis. 9. 1-4, and 10-11
Matt. 6. 33
Luke 18. 1-8

II Cor. 12. 7b-9a
Eph. 3. 14-19
6. 18
Phil. 4. 6-7
Col. 1. 9ff.
Heb. 4. 14-16
13. 3

Morning

(51) O thou, who art the true sun of the world, ever rising, and never going down; who, by thy most wholesome appearing and sight dost nourish and gladden all things in heaven and earth; we beseech thee mercifully to shine into our hearts, that the night and darkness of sin, and the mists of error on every side, being driven away by the brightness of thy shining within our hearts, we may all our life walk without stumbling, as in the day-time, and, being pure and clean from the works of darkness, may abound in all good works which thou hast prepared for us to walk in.

Erasmus (1467-1536)

(52) O God, who art the author of peace and lover of concord, in knowledge of whom standeth our eternal life, whose service is perfect freedom: defend us thy humble servants in all assaults of our enemies; that we, surely trusting in thy defence, may not fear the power of any adversaries; through the might of Jesus Christ our Lord.

Book of Common Prayer

(53) O Lord our heavenly Father, almighty and everlasting God, who hast safely brought us to the beginning of this day: defend us in the same with thy mighty power; and grant that this day we fall into no sin, neither run into any kind of danger; but that all our doings may be ordered by thy governance, to do always that is righteous in thy sight; through Jesus Christ our Lord.

Book of Common Prayer

(54) Make us remember, O God, that every day is thy gift, and ought to be used according to thy command; through Jesus Christ our Lord.

Samuel Johnson (1709-84)

(55) Lord, wake me by thy calling.
lead me to thy light;
feed me with thy love;
and speed me on thy service;
to-day and for ever.

Christian Faith and Practice

Evening

(56) Look down, O Lord, from thy heavenly throne, illuminate the darkness of this night with thy celestial brightness, and from the sons of light banish the deeds of darkness; through Jesus Christ our Lord.

Ambrosian Sacramentary (5th Century)

(57) O God, from whom all holy desires, all good counsels, and all just works do proceed, give unto thy servants that peace which the world cannot give; that both, our hearts may be set to obey thy commandments and also, that by thee we being defended from the fear of our enemies may pass our time in rest and quietness; through the merits of Jesus Christ our Saviour.

Gelasian Sacramentary, 5th-7th Century
(Book of Common Prayer)

(58) Lighten our darkness, we beseech thee, O Lord; and by thy great mercy defend us from all perils and dangers of this night, for the love of thy only Son, our Saviour, Jesus Christ.

Gelasian Sacramentary (Book of Common Prayer)

(59) Be present, O merciful God, and protect us through the silent hours of this night, so that we who are wearied by the changes and chances of this fleeting world may repose upon thine eternal changelessness; through Jesus Christ our Lord.

Gelasian Sacramentary

(60) O LORD GOD, who hast been pleased to create the night for the repose of man, as thou dost appoint unto him the day for labour, grant unto us so to rest this night in the body that our souls may be awake to thee and may be uplifted in thy love: grant that we may cast off all earthly cares, but that the thought of thy goodness and thy grace may be ever present to our minds, that while our bodies rest our consciences may find spiritual repose. May it please thee to keep us pure both in body and in spirit, that even our sleep may be to the glory of thy name. And since, being but poor sinners, we have not passed this day without offending against thee in various ways, we beseech thee that as all is now hidden by the darkness which thou sendest on the earth, so thou wouldest be pleased to bury our faults by thy compassion, so that we may not be separated from thy face. Hear us, our God, our Father and Saviour, through our Lord Jesus Christ.

Jean Calvin and Theodore de Beza
(*Strasbourg* 1539)

(61) O Lord our God, refresh us with quiet sleep when we are wearied with the day's work; that being assisted with the help which our weakness needs, we may be devoted to thee both in body and mind: through Jesus Christ our Lord.

Leonine Sacramentary (*5th-7th Century*)

(62) Save us, O Lord, waking, and guard us sleeping, that awake we may watch with Christ, and asleep we may rest in peace.

Compline

(63) Abide with us, Lord, for it is toward evening and the day is far spent. Abide with us and with thy whole Church. Abide with us in the end of the day, in the end of our life, in the end of the world. Abide with us with thy grace and bounty, with thy holy word and sacrament, with thy comfort and thy blessing. Abide with us when over us cometh the night of affliction and fear, the night of doubt and temptation, the night of bitter death. Abide with us and with all thy faithful, through time and eternity.

Löhe (1808-1872)

(64) O almighty Father, who in thy divine mercy, dost cover the earth with the curtain of darkness, that all the weary may rest; grant to us, and to all men, rest in thee this night. Let thy grace, we beseech thee, comfort and support all that are to spend it in sorrow, in affliction, or in fear. We commend into thy hands ourselves, with all our dear relations, friends and neighbours. Strengthen and confirm thy faithful people; convert the wicked, arouse the careless, recover the fallen, relieve the sick, give peace to the dying and remove all hindrances to the advancement of thy truth, that thy holy name may be glorified in Jesus Christ our Lord and Saviour.

Daily Services

Guidance

(65) O God, who art the light of the minds that know thee, the life of the souls that love thee, and the strength of the wills that seek thee; help us so to know

thee that we may truly love thee; so to love thee that we may fully serve thee, whose service is perfect freedom; through Jesus Christ our Lord.

Gelasian Sacramentary

(66) Eternal Light, shine into our hearts,
Eternal Goodness, deliver us from evil,
Eternal Power, be our support,
Eternal Wisdom, scatter the darkness of our ignorance,
Eternal Pity, have mercy upon us;
that with all our heart and mind and soul and strength we may seek thy face and be brought by thine infinite mercy to thy holy presence; through Jesus Christ our Lord.

Alcuin (735-804)

(67) O Lord, Jesus Christ, who art the way, the truth and the life, we pray thee suffer us not to stray from thee who art the way, nor to distrust thee who art the truth, nor to rest in any other thing than thee, who art the life. Teach us by thy Holy Spirit what to believe, what to do and wherein to take our rest. For thy name's sake we ask it.

Erasmus (1467-1536)

(68) O Lord, we beseech thee mercifully to receive the prayers of thy people which call upon thee: and grant that they may both perceive and know what things they ought to do, and also may have grace and power faithfully to fulfil the same; through Jesus Christ our Lord.

Book of Common Prayer

(69) O God, forasmuch as without thee we are not able to please thee; mercifully grant, that thy Holy Spirit may in all things direct and rule our hearts; through Jesus Christ our Lord.

Book of Common Prayer

(70) Guide us, O Lord, in all the changes and varieties of the world, that we may have evenness and tranquillity of spirit: that we may not murmur in adversity, nor in prosperity wax proud, but in serene faith resign our souls to thy divine will; through Jesus Christ our Lord.

After Jeremy Taylor (1613-1667)

(71) Lord, lift thou up the light of thy countenance upon us,
that in thy light we may see light,
the light of thy grace to-day,
the light of glory hereafter;
through Jesus Christ our Lord.

Lancelot Andrewes (1555-1626)

(72) Be, Lord,
within me to strengthen me,
without me to preserve me,
over me to shelter me,
beneath me to support me,
before me to direct me,
behind me to bring me back,
round about me to fortify me.

Lancelot Andrewes (1555-1626)

(73) Almighty God, the giver of all good things, without whose help all labour is insufficient, and without whose grace all wisdom is folly; grant, we beseech thee, that in this our undertaking, thy Holy Spirit may not be withheld from us, but that we may promote thy glory, and the coming of thy Kingdom. Grant this, O Lord, for the sake of Jesus Christ.

Samuel Johnson (1750)

(74) O God, by whom the meek are guided in judgment, and light riseth up in darkness for the godly; grant us, in our doubts and uncertainties, the grace to ask what thou wouldst have us to do; that the Spirit of wisdom may save us from false choices, and that in thy light we may see light, and in thy straight path may not stumble; through Jesus Christ our Lord.

William Bright (*19th Century*)

(75) Almighty God, who hast sent the Spirit of truth unto us to guide us into all truth, so rule our lives by thy power, that we may be truthful in word, and deed, and thought. Keep us, most merciful Saviour with thy gracious protection, that no fear or hope may ever make us false in act or speech. Cast out from us whatsoever loveth or maketh a lie, and bring us all into the perfect freedom of thy truth; through Jesus Christ thy Son our Lord.

Bishop Westcott (*19th Century*)

(76) Make us wise, O Lord,
To know what it befits us to know,
That we may do what thou wouldest have us do,
And be what thou wouldest have us be;
For Jesus Christ's sake.

G. W. Briggs

Temptation

(77) O God, who knowest us to be set in the midst of so many and great dangers, that by reason of the frailty of our nature we cannot always stand upright, grant to us such strength and protection as may support us in all dangers, and carry us through all temptations; through Jesus Christ our Lord.

Gelasian Sacramentary (Book of Common Prayer)

(78) Good Jesu, who didst vouchsafe to be tempted as we; to overcome Satan for us and in us; teach the tempted swiftly to hold thee; hold them lest they fall; raise them, if they give way; cheer them, if they despond; make them to hold tighter to thee; and never let us for an instant let thee go, until thou bless us; for thine own name's sake we ask it.

E. B. Pusey (19th Century)

The Fruit of the Spirit

Love

(79) O God, who hast prepared for them that love thee such good things as pass man's understanding; pour into our hearts such love towards thee, that we, loving thee above all things, may obtain thy promises, which

exceed all that we can desire; through Jesus Christ our Lord.

Gelasian Sacramentary (Book of Common Prayer)

(80) O Lord, who hast taught us that all our doings without charity are nothing worth: send thy Holy Ghost, and pour into our hearts that most excellent gift of charity, the very bond of peace and of all virtues, without which whosoever liveth is counted dead before thee: grant this for thine only Son Jesus Christ's sake.

Book of Common Prayer

(81) Almighty and most merciful Father, who hast given us a new commandment that we should love one another, give us also grace that we may fulfil it. Make us gentle, courteous and forbearing. Direct our lives so that we may look each to the good of the other in word and deed. And hallow all our friendships by the blessing of thy Spirit; for his sake who loved us, and gave himself for us, Jesus Christ our Lord.

Bishop Westcott (19th Century)

(82) Blessed Lord, who for our sakes was content to bear sorrow, and want and death, grant unto us such a measure of thy Spirit that we may follow thee in all self-denial and tenderness of soul. Help us by thy great love to succour the afflicted, to relieve the needy and destitute, to share the burdens of the heavy laden, and ever to see thee in all who are poor and desolate, for thine own name's sake.

Bishop Westcott (19th Century)

(83) O God, the God of all goodness and of all grace, who art worthy of a greater love than we can either give or understand; fill our hearts, we beseech thee, with such love toward thee that nothing may seem too hard for us to do or to suffer in obedience to thy will; and grant that thus loving thee, we may become daily more like unto thee, and finally obtain the crown of life which thou hast promised to those that love thee; through Jesus Christ our Lord.

Bishop Westcott (19th Century)

(84) O God, mercifully grant unto me that the fire of thy love may burn up in me all things that displease thee, and make me meet for thy heavenly kingdom.

P.P.

Joy

(85) O Lord, renew our spirits and draw our hearts unto thyself, that our work may not be to us a burden, but a delight; and give us such a mighty love to thee as may sweeten all our obedience. O, let us not serve thee with the spirit of bondage as slaves, but with the cheerfulness and gladness of children, delighting ourselves in thee and rejoicing in thy work; through Jesus Christ our Lord.

Benjamin Jenks (1664)

(86) O almighty God, who alone canst order the unruly wills and affections of sinful men: grant unto thy people, that they may love the thing which thou commandest, and desire that which thou dost promise; that so, among the sundry and manifold changes of

the world, our hearts may surely there be fixed, where true joys are to be found; through Jesus Christ our Lord.

Book of Common Prayer

(87) O God, the strength of them that labour and the rest of the weary: grant us when we are tired with our work to be re-created by thy Spirit; that being renewed for the service of thy kingdom, we may serve thee gladly in freshness of body and mind; through Jesus Christ our Lord.

The Kingdom, the Power and the Glory

Peace

(88) O God, who art peace everlasting, whose chosen reward is the gift of peace, and who hast taught us that the peacemakers are thy children; pour thy peace into our souls, that everything discordant may utterly vanish, and all that makes for peace be loved and sought by us always; through Jesus Christ our Lord.

Mozarabic Sacramentary

(89) Lord, make us instruments of thy peace.
Where there is hatred, let us sow love;
where there is injury, pardon;
where there is discord, union;
where there is doubt, faith;
where there is despair, hope;
where there is darkness, light;
where there is sadness, joy;
for thy mercy and for thy truth's sake.

St. Francis of Assisi

Longsuffering, Perseverance, Patience

(90) O most merciful redeemer, friend and brother,
may we
know thee more clearly,
love thee more dearly,
and follow thee more nearly,
for thine own sake.

St. Richard, Bishop of Chichester
(13th Century)

(91) O Lord God, when thou givest to thy servants to endeavour any great matter, grant us also to know that it is not the beginning, but the continuing of the same unto the end, until it be thoroughly finished, which yieldeth the true glory; through him who for the finishing of thy work laid down his life, our redeemer, Jesus Christ.

After Sir Francis Drake

(92) O God, the protector of all that trust in thee, without whom nothing is strong, nothing is holy: Increase and multiply upon us thy mercy; that, thou being our ruler and guide, we may so pass through things temporal, that we finally lose not the things eternal: grant this, O heavenly Father, for Jesus Christ's sake our Lord.

Book of Common Prayer

(93) O everlasting God, who from all eternity dost behold and order all things, and hast called us to serve thee in this our generation, doing the work of God

after the manner of men: enable us to use the talents entrusted to us, to thy glory and the service of others, that at the last we may hear that most joyful voice, Well done, thou good and faithful servant, enter thou into the joy of thy Lord; through the same our Saviour Jesus Christ.

From Jeremy Taylor

(94) Almighty God, whose beloved Son, for our sake, willingly offered himself to endure the cross, its agony and its shame: remove from us all coldness and cowardice and give us courage to take up our cross and follow him; through the same Jesus Christ our Lord.

G. W. Briggs

(95) Lord of the harvest, who dost sow good seed into the hearts of all men: grant that our hearts may not be so hardened by the world's traffic that the seed can take no root; nor so shallow that the roots can find no depth; nor so cumbered with the cares and riches of the world that the growing shoots are choked; but that we may be good ground, bearing good fruit; to the glory of thy name.

G. W. Briggs

(96) Bless, us, O God, with the vision of thy being and beauty, that in the strength of it we may work without haste and without sloth: through Jesus Christ our Lord.

Book of Prayers for Students

(97) Almighty God, give us grace to be not only hearers but doers of thy holy word, not only to admire but to obey thy doctrine, not only to profess but to practise thy religion, not only to love but to live thy gospel. So grant that what we learn of thy glory we may receive into our hearts and show forth in our lives, through Jesus Christ our Lord.

Prayers for the Lambeth Conference, 1948

Suffering

(98) Almighty God, who hast shown us in the life and teaching of thy Son the true way of blessedness, thou hast also showed us in his suffering and death that the path of love may lead to the cross, and the reward of faithfulness may be a crown of thorns. Give us grace to learn these hard lessons. May we take up our cross and follow Christ in the strength of patience and the constancy of faith; and may we have such fellowship with him in his sorrow that we may know the secret of his strength and peace, and see even in our darkest hour the shining of the eternal light, for his sake who died and rose again for us, the same Jesus Christ our Lord.

John Hunter (19th Century)

(99) O Almighty God, who having begun in me (us) a good work wilt perform it until the day of Jesus Christ, grant that my (our) love may abound yet more and more in knowledge and in all judgment, that I (we) may approve things that are excellent, that I (we) may be sincere and without offence, being filled

with the fruits of righteousness which are by Jesus Christ, unto the glory and praise of God.

Based on Philippians I (Book of Prayers for Students)

Gentleness

(100) Set a watch, O Lord, upon our tongue;
that we may never speak the cruel word which is untrue;
or, being true, is not the whole truth;
or, being wholly true, is merciless;
for the love of Jesus Christ our Lord.

G. W. Briggs

(101) O Lord Jesus Christ, whose unjust condemnation we justly condemn: save us from all malice and uncharitableness in accusing our brethren, lest what we do unto others, we do unto thee, and crucify thee afresh, our saviour, our lover, our lord, for ever and ever.

E. Milner White

Goodness

(102) O Lord God, who with life itself hast bestowed on each of thy children his own good gifts: take from me all envy and jealousy of the gifts bestowed upon others; and grant me to make increase of my own by devoting them, in true thankfulness toward thee, to the happiness of all around, for the sake of Jesus Christ.

Source Unknown

Faithfulness

(103) Give me, O Lord, a steadfast heart,
which no unworthy thought can drag downwards,
an unconquered heart, which no tribulation can wear out;
an upright heart, which no unworthy purpose may tempt aside.
Bestow upon me also, O Lord my God,
understanding to know thee,
diligence to seek thee,
wisdom to find thee,
and a faithfulness that may finally embrace thee;
through Jesus Christ our Lord.

St. Thomas Aquinas (1225-1274)

(104) O God, speak to our hearts when men faint for fear, and the love of many grows cold, and there is distress of the nations upon earth. Keep us resolute and steadfast in the things that cannot be shaken, abounding in hope and knowing that our labour is not in vain in thee. Restore our faith in the omnipotence of good; renew the love which never faileth; and make us to lift up our eyes and behold, beyond the things which are seen and temporal, the things which are unseen and eternal.

Free Church Book of Common Prayer

(105) Set free, O Lord, the souls of thy servants from all restlessness and anxiety; give us that peace and power which flow from thee and keep us in all per-

plexities and distresses, in all griefs and grievances from any fear or faithlessness, that so upheld by thy strength and stayed on the rock of thy faithfulness, through storm and stress we may abide in thee.

Book of Prayers for Students

Meekness

(106) O God, help me not to despise or oppose what I do not understand.

William Penn (1644-1718)

(107) O Lord God, holy and almighty, let our pride be that we are members of Christ, our praise be not of men but of thee, and our memorial that our names be written in heaven; for Jesus Christ's sake.

Adapted from Christina Rosetti

(108) Lord Jesus Christ, who by thy precept and example hast taught us that the greatest of all is the servant of all, and that the humble shall be exalted; make us content to take with gladness the lower place and if it shall please thee to call us higher, do thou preserve within us a simple and humble heart; to thy great glory.

G. W. Briggs

Temperance or Discipline

(109) Defend me, O Lord, against idleness and the misuse of time lest my life be unprofitable to thee, mischievous to others, and without honour or joy to myself. In Christ's name I ask it.

(110) Lord Christ, who for my sake didst become poor, though thou wast rich: help me to use my money rightly, wisely, and generously, that having used corruptible goods to thy glory, I may at last gain the inheritance incorruptible, where thou livest and reignest with the Father and the Holy Spirit, one God, world without end.

(111) O God, help us to be masters of ourselves that we may become the servants of others, and thus follow in the path of thy blessed Son, Jesus Christ our Lord.

Alec Paterson

(112) O God, grant that I may practise such temperance in meat, drink and sleep, and all bodily enjoyments as may fit me for the duties to which thou shalt call me, and by thy blessing procure me freedom of thought and quietness of mind, that I may so serve thee in this short and frail life, that I may be received by thee at my death to everlasting happiness. Take not, O Lord, thy Holy Spirit from me, deliver me not up to vain fears, but have mercy on me, for the sake of Jesus Christ our Lord.

Samuel Johnson (18th Century)

At Study

(113) Almighty God, our heavenly Father, without whose help labour is useless, without whose light search is vain, invigorate my studies, and direct my inquiries, that I may by due diligence and right discernment establish myself and others in thy holy faith.

Take not, O Lord, thy Holy Spirit from me; let not evil thoughts have dominion in my mind. Let me not linger in ignorance, but enlighten and support me, for the sake of Jesus Christ our Lord.

Samuel Johnson (18th Century)

(114) O Lord, my maker and protector, who hast graciously sent me into this world, to work out my salvation, enable me to drive from me all such unquiet thoughts as may mislead or hinder me in the practice of those duties which thou hast required. When I behold the works of thy hands and consider the course of thy providence, give me grace always to remember that thy thoughts are not my thoughts, nor thy ways my ways. And while it shall please thee to continue me in this world where much is to be done and little to be known, teach me by thy Holy Spirit to withdraw my mind from unprofitable and dangerous inquiries, from difficulties vainly curious, and doubts impossible to be solved. Let me rejoice in the light which thou hast imparted, let me serve thee with active zeal, and humble confidence, and wait with patient expectation for the time in which the soul which thou receivest, shall be satisfied with knowledge. Grant this, O Lord, for Jesus Christ's sake.

Samuel Johnson (18th Century)

(115) Almighty God, who hast sent the Spirit of truth unto us to guide us into all truth, so rule our lives by thy power, that we may be truthful in word and deed and thought. O keep us, most merciful Saviour, with

thy gracious protection, that no fear or hope may ever make us false in act or speech. Cast out from us whatsoever loveth or maketh a lie, and bring us all into the perfect freedom of thy truth; through Jesus Christ our Lord.

Bishop Westcott (19th Century)

Before Sitting for an Examination

(116) O Lord God, in whom we live and move and have our being; open our eyes that we may behold thy fatherly presence ever about us. Draw our hearts to thee with the power of thy love. Teach us to be anxious for nothing; and when we have done what thou hast given us to do, help us, O God, our Saviour, to leave the issue to thy wisdom.

Bishop Westcott (19th Century)

(117) God of truth, who hast guided men in knowledge throughout the ages, and from whom every good thought cometh, help us in our study to use thy gifts of wisdom and knowledge. Let us read good books carefully, and listen to all wise teaching humbly, that we may be led into all truth, and strengthened in all goodness of life, to the praise of thy holy name.

Rowland Williams (19th Century, adapted)

(118) Dispel, O Lord, O Father of light, all clouds of doubt and the darkness about our earthly course; that in thy light we may see light, and come both to know thee as we are known, and to love thee as we are loved; through Jesus Christ our Lord.

(119) Be present, we beseech thee, most Holy Spirit, in all our studies, researches and undertakings, that by thine almighty aid we may both know and do the truth.

S. P. T. Prideaux

(120) Grant, O Lord, we pray thee, that as we seek for truth we may find that the search leads us to thyself. Give us courage to seek honestly and reverence to seek humbly; and when our minds are perplexed, and we cannot find thee, give us patience to go on with our daily duties; through Jesus Christ our Lord.

Book of Prayers for Students

(121) Do thou give us, O Holy Spirit of God, a new mind to comprehend thy loving purposes, a new heart to rejoice in them, and a new perseverance upon the paths of thy will, now and for ever.

(122) O Eternal God, who hast made all things for men, and men for thy glory, sanctify our bodies and souls, our thoughts and our intentions, our words and our actions, that whatever we shall think, or speak, or do, may be designed to the glory of thy name; and by thy blessing may be effective and successful in the work of God. Lord, turn our necessities into virtues, the works of nature into the works of grace, by making them orderly, temperate, subordinate, and profitable to ends beyond their own efficacy. And let no pride or self-seeking, no covetousness or revenge, no little ends and low imaginations, pollute our spirits,

and unhallow any of our words and actions; but let our bodies be the servants of our spirits, and both body and spirit servants of Jesus, that, doing all things for thy glory here, we may be partakers of thy glory hereafter, through Jesus Christ our Lord.

Adapted from Jeremy Taylor

(123) Teach us, O God, the love that is revealed in Jesus Christ, that we may be instructed unto thy kingdom. Grant us the graces of humility and of an inquiring mind, and by thy Spirit guide us into all truth. As we seek to share in the passion of the mind of Christ, give us grace that, bearing in our minds the division and sin of the world, we may know in Christ the redemption wherein all things are made one. This we ask in his name.

(124) Deliver us, O God, from following the fashions of the day in our thinking. Save us from the worship of power, whether power over nature or power over men; save us from the worship of science, and grant that, giving thee thanks for the skill of the scientist, we may be preserved from the abuse of his discoveries. Help us never to confuse any creature with the Creator, or man with God. May we acknowledge man's reason as thy gift and, being freed from all false hopes and misplaced trust, find in thee our hope and our salvation, through Jesus Christ our Lord.

(125) O everlasting God, who by thy Holy Spirit dost lead men to the knowledge of the truth: inspire, we

pray thee, all who teach and all who learn; that they may have zeal to seek the truth, right judgment to discern it, wisdom to understand it, resolution to hold it fast, and faith to act upon it. Guide them in doubt and perplexity, deliver them from carelessness or irreverence, lest thy word be heard and not heeded, believed and not obeyed, known and not lived; that all men may know thee the only true God, and him whom thou didst send, even Jesus Christ our Lord.

New Every Morning

In an S.C.M. Branch

(126) O Lord Jesus Christ, who didst say to thy disciples, Come ye apart and rest awhile: grant, we beseech thee, to thy servants now gathered together so to seek thee, whom our souls desire to love, that we may both find thee and be found of thee; and grant such love and such wisdom to accompany the words which shall be spoken in thy name, that they may not fall to the ground, but may lead us onward to thy perfect service; who livest and reignest, God, for ever and ever.

Adapted from R. M. Benson

(127) Almighty God, without whom nothing is strong and nothing is holy, may our speaking and hearing at this time be to the increase of faith, hope and love. May all that is untrue perish in the speaking, and all that is true be preserved for our use and thy service: through Jesus Christ our Lord.

John Hunter (*adapted*)

(128) Lord, take our minds and think through them; take our lips and speak through them; take our hearts and set them on fire with the desire to do thy holy will, in the name of Jesus Christ our Lord.

W. H. Aitken (adapted)

(129) May the Spirit, O Lord, who proceedeth from thee, enlighten our minds and, as thy Son hath promised, lead us unto all truth; through the same our Lord Jesus Christ.

Bible Study (see Intercession Nos. 159-162).

Dedication

(130) O thou who hast taught us that we are most truly free when we lose our wills in thine, help us to gain that liberty by continual surrender unto thee, that we may walk in the way which thou hast prepared for us, and in doing thy will may find our life through Jesus Christ our Lord.

Gelasian Sacramentary

(131) God be in my head and in my understanding;
God be in my eyes and in my looking;
God be in my mouth and in my speaking;
God be in my heart and in my thinking;
God be at mine end and at my departing.

Sarum Primer, 1558

(132) Teach us, good Lord, to serve thee as thou deservest; to give and not to count the cost; to fight

and not to heed the wounds; to toil and not to seek for rest; to labour and not to ask for any reward, save that of knowing that we do thy will, through Jesus Christ our Lord.

St. Ignatius Loyola (1491-1556)

(133) Remember, O Lord, what thou hast wrought in us, and not what we deserve; and as thou hast called us to thy service, make us worthy of our calling: through Jesus Christ our Lord.

National Prayers, 1914

(134) O thou in whom we live and move and have our being, we offer and present unto thee ourselves, our souls and our bodies, our thoughts and our desires, our words and our deeds, to be a reasonable, holy and living sacrifice unto thee; through Jesus Christ our Lord.

Based on Acts 17. 28 and Romans 12. 1 and 2

(135) Grant us, O Lord,
in thought, faith;
in word, wisdom;
in deed, courage;
in life, service:
through Jesus Christ our Lord.

Inscription on a column in front of the Viceroy's House in New Delhi

INTERCESSION

General

(136) In peace let us pray to the Lord.
For the peace which is from above, and for the salvation of our souls, let us pray to the Lord.

R. (after each petition) *Lord, have mercy upon us.*

For the peace of the whole world, for the good estate of the holy churches of God and for the union of all, let us pray to the Lord.
For this holy house, and for those who with faith, reverence, and godly fear enter therein, let us pray to the Lord.
For our homes that they may be holy, and for all our pastors, teachers and rulers, let us pray to the Lord.
For this city and country, and for all who dwell therein, let us pray to the Lord.
For temperate weather, abundance of fruits of the earth, and for peaceful seasons, let us pray to the Lord.
For those who travel by land, by air or by water; for the sick and the suffering; for prisoners and captives, and their preservation, let us pray to the Lord.
For our deliverance from all afflictions, strife and necessity, let us pray to the Lord.
Protect us, save us, have mercy upon us, and preserve us, O God, by thy grace. We commend ourselves,

and one another, and our whole life unto Christ our God. For all glory, honour and worship befits thee, the Father, the Son and the Holy Ghost, now and for ever and world without end.

The Litany of Peace (adapted from the Divine Liturgy of St. John Chrysostom)

(137) O God, the creator and preserver of all mankind, we humbly beseech thee for all sorts and conditions of men; that thou wouldest be pleased to make thy ways known unto them, thy saving health unto all nations. More especially, we pray for the good estate of the Catholick Church; that it may be so guided and governed by thy good Spirit, that all who profess and call themselves Christians may be led into the way of truth, and hold the faith in unity of spirit, in the bond of peace, and in righteousness of life. Finally, we commend to thy fatherly goodness all those who are any ways afflicted, or distressed, in mind, body or estate (*especially* . . .) that it may please thee to comfort and relieve them, according to their several necessities, giving them patience under their sufferings and a happy issue out of all their afflictions. And this we beg for Jesus Christ his sake.

Book of Common Prayer

(138) O God of infinite mercy, who hast compassion on all men, hear the prayers of thy servants, who are unworthy to ask any petition for themselves, yet are in duty bound to pray for others: let thy mercy descend upon the Church; preserve her in peace and

truth, in unity and service; that her sacrifice of prayer and thanksgiving may ever ascend to thy throne. In mercy remember the king; keep him perpetually in thy fear and favour; and grant that all who bear office under him may serve with a single eye to thy glory. Remember our friends, all that have done us good; return their kindness double.

Forgive our enemies; and help us to forgive, as we hope to be forgiven. Comfort the afflicted; speak peace to troubled consciences; strengthen the weak; confirm the strong; instruct the ignorant; deliver the oppressed; relieve the needy; and bring us all by the waters of comfort and in the ways of righteousness to thy eternal kingdom; through Jesus Christ our Lord.

After Jeremy Taylor

A Bidding Prayer before a Christmas Carol Service

(139) Beloved in Christ, be it this Christmastide our care and delight to prepare ourselves to hear again the message of the angels, and in heart and mind to go even unto Bethlehem, and see this thing which is come to pass, and the babe lying in a manger.

Let us read and mark in Holy Scripture the tale of the loving purposes of God from the first days of our disobedience unto the glorious redemption brought us by this holy child: and let us make this place glad with our carols of praise.

But first let us pray for the needs of his whole world; for peace and goodwill over all the earth; for unity and brotherhood within the Church he came to build, and especially in the Commonwealth of our sovereign lord king George; and within this city (town, village), and university (college, hall).

And because this of all things would rejoice his heart, let us at this time remember in his name the poor and the helpless, the cold, the hungry, and the oppressed; the sick and them that mourn; the lonely and the unloved; the aged and the little children; all those who know not the Lord Jesus, or who love him not, or who by sin have grieved his heart of love.

Lastly, let us remember before God all those who rejoice with us, but upon another shore and in a greater light, that multitude which no man can number, whose hope was in the Word made flesh, and with whom, in this Lord Jesus, we for evermore are one.

These prayers and praises let us humbly offer up to the throne of heaven, in the words which Christ himself hath taught us:

Our Father . . .

The almighty God bless us with his grace: Christ give us the joys of everlasting life: and unto the fellowship of the citizens above may the King of angels bring us all.

Daily Prayer (*adapted, by permission, from the service at King's College, Cambridge*)

The Church

General

(140) Remember, O Lord, thy Church, to deliver her from all evil, and to make her perfect in thy love; and gather together from the four winds the sanctified Church into thy kingdom, which thou hast prepared

for her. For thine is the power and the glory for evermore.

The Didache (2nd Century)

(141) O God of unchangeable power and eternal light, look favourably on thy whole Church, that wonderful and sacred mystery; and by the operation of thy providence, carry out the work of man's salvation; and let the whole world feel and see that things which were cast down are being raised up, that those things which had grown old are being made new, and that all things are returning to perfection through him from whom they took their origin, even through our Lord Jesus Christ.

Gelasian Sacramentary

(142) We beseech thee, O Lord, to guide thy Church with thy perpetual governance that it may walk warily in times of quiet, and boldly in times of trouble, through Jesus Christ our Lord.

Franciscan Breviary (13th Century)

(143) Gracious Father, we humbly beseech thee for thy holy catholic Church. Fill it with all truth; in all truth with all peace. Where it is corrupt, purge it; where it is in error, direct it; where it is superstitious, rectify it; where anything is amiss, reform it; where it is right, strengthen and confirm it; where it is in want, furnish it; where it is divided and rent asunder, make up the breaches of it, O thou holy one of Israel, for the sake of Jesus Christ our Lord and Saviour.

Archbishop Laud (1573-1645)

(144) O God, our shepherd, give to the Church a new vision and charity, new wisdom and fresh understanding, the revival of her brightness and the renewal of her unity; that the eternal message of thy Son, undefiled by the traditions of men, may be hailed as the good news of the new age; through him who maketh all things new, Jesus Christ our Lord.

Percy Dearmer (20th Century)

Her Unity

(145) Eternal and merciful God, who art the God of peace and not of discord: have mercy upon thy Church, divided in thy service; and grant that we, seeking unity in Christ, and in the truth of thy holy word, with one mind and one mouth may glorify thee, the Father of our Lord Jesus Christ.

Lancelot Andrewes (Preces Privatae, 17th Century)

(146) O God, the Father of our Lord Jesus Christ, our only saviour, the prince of peace: give us grace to lay to heart the dangers we are in by our divisions. Take away all hatred and prejudice, and whatsoever else may hinder us from godly union and concord; that as there is but one body, and one Spirit, and one hope of our calling, one Lord, one faith, one baptism, one God and Father of us all, so we may henceforth be all of one heart, and of one soul, united in one holy bond of truth and peace, of faith and charity, and may, with one mind and one mouth, glorify thee; through Jesus Christ our Lord.

Book of Common Prayer (Accession Service, 1714)

(147) O Lord Jesus Christ, who didst say to thine apostles, Peace I leave with you, my peace I give unto you: regard not our sins, but the faith of thy Church, and grant it that peace and unity which is agreeable to thy will; who livest and reignest with the Father and the Holy Spirit, one God, world without end.

Roman Missal

(148) Let us give thanks for the gifts and graces of each great division of Christendom:

For the ROMAN CATHOLIC CHURCH; its glorious traditions, its disciplines in holiness, its worship, rich with the religious passion of the centuries; its noble company of martyrs, doctors and saints;

We thank Thee, O Lord, and bless Thy Holy Name (repeated after each item).

For the EASTERN ORTHODOX CHURCH; its secret treasure of mystic experience; its marvellous liturgy; its regard for the collective life and its common will as a source of authority;

For the great PROTESTANT COMMUNIONS;

For the CONGREGATIONALIST jealousy for the rightful independence of the soul and of the group;

For the stress in the BAPTIST CHURCHES upon personal regeneration and upon the conscious relation of the mature soul to its Lord;

For the power of the METHODISTS to awaken the conscience of Christians to our social evils; and for their emphasis upon the witness of personal experience, and upon the power of the disciplined life;

For the PRESBYTERIAN reverence for the sovereignty of

God and their confidence in his faithfulness to his covenant; for their sense of the moral law, expressing itself in constitutional government;
For the witness to the perpetual real presence of the inner light in every human soul borne by the Religious SOCIETY OF FRIENDS and for their faithful continuance of a free prophetic ministry;
For the LUTHERAN CHURCH; its devotion to the grace of God and the word of God, enshrined in the ministry of the word and sacraments;
For the ANGLICAN CHURCH; its reverent and temperate ways, through its Catholic heritage and its Protestant conscience; its yearning concern over the divisions of Christendom, and its longing to be used as a house of reconciliation.

Federal Council of Churches Bulletin
U.S.A. 1940

(149) O God of peace, who through thy Son Jesus Christ didst set forth one faith for the salvation of mankind: Send thy grace and heavenly blessing upon all Christian people who are striving to draw nearer to thee and to each other, in the unity of the spirit and in the bond of peace. Give us penitence for our divisions, wisdom to know thy truth, courage to do thy will, love which shall break down the barriers of prejudice and pride, and an unswerving loyalty to thy holy name. Unite us all in thee as thou, O Father, with thy Son and the Holy Spirit, art one God, world without end.

Faith and Order Manual (*Bishop Anderson,* 1927)

Her Mission

(150) O God of all the nations of the earth, remember the multitudes of the heathen who, though created in thine image, have not known thee nor the dying of thy Son their saviour Jesus Christ; and grant that by the prayers and labours of thy Church they may be delivered from all superstition and unbelief, and brought to worship thee; through him whom thou hast sent to be the resurrection and the life of all men, the same thy Son, Jesus Christ our Lord.

St. Francis Xavier (trs. E. Milner-White)

(151) O God, who hast made of one blood all nations of men to dwell on the face of the earth, and didst send thy blessed Son to preach peace to them that are far off, and to them that are nigh; grant that all the peoples of the world may feel after thee and find thee; and hasten, O Lord, the fulfilment of thy promise to pour out thy Spirit upon all flesh; through Jesus Christ our Lord.

Bishop Cotton (19th Century)

(152) O Heavenly Father, we pray thee to bless and protect thy servants who have gone forth to preach the gospel in distant lands (*especially* . . .); give them such success in their labours that thy way may be known upon earth, thy saving health among all nations. Hear and grant this our prayer, O God, for the sake of Jesus Christ, our blessed Lord and Saviour.

Family Prayer of the Church of Ireland

(153) O Father of light and God of all truth, purge the whole world from all errors, abuses, corruptions and

sins. Abolish the reign of sin and establish the kingdom of grace in all hearts. Let humility triumph over pride and ambition; charity over hatred, envy and malice; purity and self-control over lust and excess; meekness over passion; and disinterestedness and poverty of spirit over covetousness and the love of this world. Let the Gospel of Christ in faith and practice prevail throughout the world, through him who liveth and reigneth with thee and the Holy Spirit, one God world without end.

Percy Dearmer (20th Century)

(154) Let us pray for Christians in temptation:
Those who receive the word with gladness, but in time of temptation fall away:
Those whose spiritual life is choked by materialism, by the cares and pleasures of this world:
Those whose faith is not strong enough to withstand the ridicule and antagonism of non-believers:
Those Church members who do not persevere and lapse into secularism:
Those who are tempted to fall back into their primitive religion of fear and the propitiation of angry deities:
Lord Jesus, we pray thee for our fellow-Christians in all parts of the world and in this land who are facing difficulties, and who are tempted to turn back because the way is hard. Make them brave and steadfast, and may their loyal witness draw others to thee; for thine own name's sake.

Prayers of the World-Wide Church (adapted)

The Ministry

(155) Almighty God, the giver of all good gifts, who of thy divine providence hast appointed divers orders in thy Church: Give thy grace, we humbly beseech thee, to all those who are (*to be*) called to any office and administration in the same; and so replenish them with the truth of thy doctrine, and endue them with innocency of life, that they may faithfully serve before thee, to the glory of thy great name, and the benefit of thy holy Church; through Jesus Christ our Lord.

Book of Common Prayer

(156) Almighty God, who hast set in thy Church some with gifts to teach and help and administer, in diversity of operation but of the same Spirit: grant to all such, we beseech thee, grace to wait on the ministry which they have received in the body of Christ with simplicity, diligence, and cheerfulness; that none think of himself more highly than he ought to think, and none seek another man's calling, but rather to be found faithful over a few things, and to receive praise of Christ in his own work. That through the effectual working in the measure of every part the whole body may be joined together and compacted, and make increase to the edifying of itself in love. To the glory of thy name in Christ Jesus our Lord.

H. J. Wotherspoon

Christians in Foreign Lands
Christians from Abroad

(157) Let us pray for Christians from overseas who come to this country:

That they may be drawn into the fellowship of a Christian congregation:

That they may continue faithful in the practice of their religion:

That their faith may not be shaken by the irreligion of many in this country:

O Lord our God, who art in every place, and from whom no space or distance can separate us: We pray thee for those who are far from the home of their fathers in a strange land. Grant that they may live as faithful followers of Jesus Christ, and be living members of his body which is the Church; through the same thy Son, our Lord and Saviour.

Prayers of the World-Wide Church

Christians Abroad

(158) Let us pray for our fellow countrymen settled overseas, in government, education, medical or business posts:

That they may live worthily of the name of Christian:

That they may be faithful in the observance of their religion:

That they may uphold Christian standards of conduct:

Let not thy name, we beseech thee, O God, be blasphemed through any of our countrymen who are dwelling abroad. Let their eyes be ever open to see thine image in all their fellow men. Take away all arrogance, contempt, or patronage, and grant that they may so fill the needs and understand the ideals of other nations and races, that they may help them to enter with us into the glorious liberty of the children of God; through Jesus Christ our Lord.

Prayers for the City of God

The Use of the Bible

(159) O Lord Jesus, let not thy word become a judgment upon us, that we hear it and do it not, that we know it and love it not, that we believe it and obey it not; thou who with the Father and the Holy Spirit livest and reignest, world without end.

Thomas à Kempis (1379-1471)

(160) Blessed Lord, who hast caused all holy scriptures to be written for our learning: grant that we may in such wise hear them, read, mark, learn, and inwardly digest them, that by patience and comfort of thy holy word, we may embrace and ever hold fast the blessed hope of everlasting life, which thou hast given us in our Saviour Jesus Christ.

Book of Common Prayer

(161) Almighty and most merciful God, who hast given the Bible to be the revelation of thy great love to man, and of thy power and will to save him; grant that our study of it may not be made in vain by the callousness or carelessness of our hearts, but that by it we may be confirmed in penitence, lifted to hope, made strong for service and filled with the true knowledge of thee and of thy Son Jesus Christ.

George Adam Smith

(162) Write upon our hearts, O Lord God, the lessons of thy holy word, and grant that we may all be doers of the same, and not forgetful hearers only; through Jesus Christ our Lord.

A. Campbell Fraser

The Communion of Saints

(163) O Father of all, we pray to thee for those whom we love, but see no longer, grant them thy peace; let light perpetual shine upon them; and in thy loving wisdom and almighty power work in them the good purpose of thy perfect will; through Jesus Christ our Lord.

Book of Common Prayer (1928)

(164) Grant, O Lord, to thy persecuted servants, that their conversation may be as it becometh the gospel of Christ; that they may stand fast in one spirit, with one mind striving together for the faith of the gospel; that in nothing terrified by their adversaries they may be bold on the behalf of Christ, not only to believe in him, but also to suffer for his sake; who liveth and reigneth with the Father and the Holy Ghost, one God, world without end.

Source unknown

S.C.M. and W.S.C.F.

(165) Almighty and most merciful God, we praise thee for the blessings bestowed upon the World's Student Christian Federation. We pray thee still to prosper its work. Graciously use it for the fulfilment of thy

purposes, in the evangelization of the world, the restoration of visible unity to thy Church, the establishment of peace and understanding among the nations, and the renewal of the universities by the power of thy Spirit.
Give wisdom, faith and courage to those who direct its policy; health and safety to those who travel for it; and grant that its members in all nations may be brought closer to one another in serving thee, through Jesus Christ our Lord.

Bishop P. H. Loyd (adapted)

At a Conference, Meeting or Retreat

(166) Almighty God, who at divers times and in divers manners hast spoken in time past unto our fathers, let thy word be spoken among us with power at this time, that thy servants may hear and obey, through him who is thy word made manifest, Jesus Christ our Lord.

(167) We thank thee, Father, for the conference which lies before us and which we now begin in thy name. Give us quiet in our minds, seriousness in the depths of our hearts and the carefree spirit which comes from faith in thee.
Be near to us every day with thy Word and thy Spirit. Bless those who are to instruct and speak, that their words may possess and give clarity and power. Bless our listening; give us the power of discernment and the will to understand and take to heart; and where we do not understand may we not be too proud or shy to share our difficulties with others and learn

from them. Bless our fellowship, so that we may help each other into the truth and on to thee, and live in the unity of the Spirit. Come, O Lord, and visit us. Be in the midst of us, living and saving. Let none of us escape thy call and miss thy peace. Into thy hands we commit ourselves. Bless our going out and our coming in from this time forth and for evermore.

Book of Prayers of the Swedish S.C.M., 1933 (*adapted*)

(168) O God, whose will it is that we should know the truth, and that the truth should make us free: deliver us from all prejudice and pride, give us sincerity in our questioning, honesty in our conclusions, and courage in our obedience. Let not love of the old blind us to that which is new, nor love of novelty lead us away from the things which endure; but as we seek, help us to know that we have been found, and that thou who hast called us art also working in us, and wilt continue with us to the end. This we pray through him by whom came grace and truth, even Jesus Christ thy Son our Lord.

Student Movement House and other International Student Clubs or Centres

(169) We remember before thee with thanksgiving, most merciful Lord, (*Student Movement House*). We praise thee for the generosity of those who founded it; for the devotion of those who have served it; and for the fellowship of those who have belonged

to it. Give, we beseech thee, peace and joy and love to all who now enter and go out from it, that men and women of all races may be drawn nearer to each other and to thee, to the glory of thy name, through Jesus Christ our Lord.

The Nations

(170) O God, whose righteous wisdom governs the heavens, and controls also the destinies of men; teach the rulers of the nations the things that belong to their peace. Save, Lord, by love, by prudence, and by fear, for Jesus Christ's sake.

(171) All nations are as flocks branded with thy letters, O Alpha and Omega. They are thy possession, and thou knowest best how to govern them. Everyone knows better how to govern his own possession than that of a stranger. The leaders of earthly nations govern a strange possession, for they govern what is thine. O Lord, guide the leaders of the nations, so that they may govern the people by thy holy will; that they may lead them in the way which thou dost point out; that they may turn them away from what is evil in thy sight; that they may guard them carefully as a great treasure which thou hast entrusted to them. Power is a great temptation, and few are those who can overcome it. Only those overcome it who know that they are thy servants, waiting at the footstool of thy feet. Many people misuse their power over nature, and not a few equally abuse their power over themselves and over others.

Very weak is every man, O Lord, and quick to give himself up to self-love and pride.

Out of love to thy nations, Creator, fill the leaders of the nations with fear of thy judgment. And for their sakes and their salvation, do not be wroth, O Lord, but uphold them with the spirit of strength, wisdom, and purity. May their souls be saved as they seek the salvation of thy nations, looking day and night unto thee, as the Leader of all leaders and the Lord of all lords. Have mercy on us, all-merciful, and hear our prayer.

Bishop Nicolai Velimirovic (1935)

(172) Almighty God, who hast created men for thy glory and hast in thy Son Jesus Christ opened the way by which they may enter into thy peace: open the eyes of all men to see the sovereignty of thine eternal truth and love, that, being delivered from the bondage of human vanity and corruption, they may find their freedom in obedience to thy laws and their brotherhood in the unity of thy service; through the same thy Son Jesus Christ our Lord.

Prayers for the Lambeth Conference 1948

(173) O God, who wouldest fold both heaven and earth in a single peace: let the design of thy great love lighten upon the waste of our wraths and sorrows; and give peace to thy Church, peace among nations, peace in our dwellings, and peace in our hearts; through thy Son our Saviour Jesus Christ.

Memorials upon Several Occasions

(174) O Lord our God, who hast reconciled us to thyself and to one another through the death of thy Son, and hast entrusted to us the ministry of reconciliation; keep ever before our hearts and minds the price that thou hast paid for the salvation of the world. Crucify our pride, destroy our enmities; and let the cross of thy Son bear in us all its fruits of righteousness and peace, for his sake.

Suzanne de Dietrich (1938)

This Nation

(175) O God, almighty Father, King of kings and Lord of lords; grant that the hearts and minds of all who go out as leaders before us, the statesmen, the judges, the men of learning and the men of wealth, may be so filled with the love of thy laws, and of that which is righteous and life-giving, that they may be worthy stewards of thy good and perfect gifts; through Jesus Christ our Lord.

Knights of the Garter (*14th Century*)

(176) O merciful God and Father, forasmuch as no counsel can stand, nor any can prosper, but only such as are gathered in thy name; we pray thy divine majesty so to incline the hearts of them that are elected to the high court of parliament, that their counsels may be subject in true obedience to thy holy word and will. Graft in them, we beseech thee, good minds to conceive, free liberty to speak; and grant to us all a ready and quiet consent to such wholesome laws and statutes, as may declare us to be thy people, and this

realm to be prosperously ruled by thy good guiding and defence; through Jesus Christ our Lord.

Prayers of 1585 (shortened and slightly altered)

(177) O Lord, thou God of righteousness and truth, grant to our king and his government, to members of parliament and all in positions of responsibility the guidance of thy Spirit. May they never lead the nation wrongly through love of power, desire to please, or unworthy ideals, but always love righteousness and truth; so may thy kingdom be advanced and thy name be hallowed; through Jesus Christ our Lord.

Book of Prayers for Students

(178) Almighty and everlasting God, who resistest the proud, and givest grace to the humble; grant, we beseech thee, that we may not exalt ourselves and provoke thine indignation, but bow down and receive the gifts of thy mercy; through Jesus Christ our Lord.

Archbishop William Temple (1939)

Society and Industry

(179) O God, who hast made us a royal priesthood that we might offer unto thee prayer and intercession for our fellow men, hear us we pray:

For all who labour with their hands, that they may enjoy the rewards of their industry;

For those who bear the responsibilities of leadership

and administration, that they may not use their authority and power for selfish advantage but be guided to do justice and to love mercy;

For those who have suffered in the battles of life, through the inhumanity of their fellows, their own limitations or the incomprehensible forces of evil, that they may contend against injustice without bitterness, overcome their weakness with diligence, and learn to accept with patience what cannot be altered;

For the rulers of the nations that they may act wisely and without pride, may seek to promote peace among the peoples and establish justice in our common life;

For teachers and ministers of the word, for artists and interpreters of our spiritual life, that they may rightly divide the word of truth, and not be tempted by any ignoble passion to corrupt the truth to which they are committed;

For prophets and saints, who awaken us from sloth, that they may continue to hold their torches high in a world darkened by prejudice and sin, and ever be obedient to the heavenly vision;

O God, who hast bound us together in this bundle of life, give us grace to understand how our lives depend upon the courage, the industry, the honesty and the integrity of our fellow men, that we may be mindful of their needs, grateful for their faithfulness and faithful in our responsibilities to them, through Jesus Christ our Lord.

Reinhold Niebuhr

(180) Prosper our industries, we pray thee, God most high, that our land may be full with all manner of store, and there be no complaining in our streets: and, as thy glorious Son our Lord plied tool and trade on earth, so give to all that labour pride in their work, a just reward, and joy both in supplying need and serving thee; through the same Jesus Christ our Lord.

Occasional Prayers Reconsidered

(181) O Lord Jesus Christ, who hast taught us that not one sparrow falls to the ground without our Father and that the very hairs of our head are numbered; grant that all those in industry, in social work, in local government and in the civil service, whose authority affects the lives of others, may serve the common good by judging impartially between man and man; and that neither rejoicing in power for its own sake, nor losing concern for people in administering systems, they may follow thee who didst serve thy brethren even unto death, and now livest and reignest with the Father and the Holy Spirit, one God, world without end.

The University or College

(182) Father, who hast (through many generations and by many bountiful servants) blessed this college/university for a place of faith and fruitful study; grant us likewise in it so to learn truth as to bear its light along all our ways, and so to learn Christ as ever to be found in him; who liveth and reigneth with thee and the Holy Ghost, one God, world without end.

King's College, Cambridge

(183) Let thy blessing, O Lord, rest upon our work in this college/university. Teach us to seek after truth, and enable us to attain it; but grant that as we increase in knowledge of earthly things, we may grow in knowledge of thee, whom to know is life eternal; through Jesus Christ our Lord.

Adapted Arnold of Rugby (1795-1842)

(184) God, who hast given us power to reason, experiment and discover, teach us to use these gifts aright. Help us to know our limitations, lest, claiming a monopoly of the truth, we become proud of our intellect and vain in our imaginations, through Jesus Christ our Lord.

The Academic Community

(185) O God, who hast made us to know each other and thee, enable all who study in this university (college) so to learn from each other and from thee, that we may attain our full stature in thy sight. Give to all specialists such a breadth of vision that they may not ignore or forget the other members of the community. Break down our intellectual divisions, so that we may all be one in our calling of study, and in the body of our Lord Jesus Christ.

Research

(186) O Lord Jesus Christ, who on thy cross didst overcome all the powers of darkness, guide all men who in seeking knowledge acquire power which can be used for good or evil purposes. Help them to bear

their responsibility, and in awe to recognize their stewardship; who livest and reignest, with the Father and the Holy Spirit, one God, world without end.

Particularly for the Student of Law

(187) Almighty God, the giver of wisdom, without whose help resolutions are vain, without whose blessing study is ineffectual, enable me, if it be thy will, to attain such knowledge as may qualify me to direct the doubtful, and instruct the ignorant, to prevent wrongs and terminate contentions; and grant that I may use that knowledge which I shall attain, to thy glory and my own salvation, for Jesus Christ's sake.

Examinations

(188) O God, who knowest the secrets of the heart, be with those now preparing (sitting) for examinations. Help them to face their task with calmness, confidence and courage; with wisdom, faithfulness and honesty; that they may do justice both to themselves and to their teachers, and set forth thy glory, who thyself art wisdom and truth, and the giver of knowledge, and of every virtue and good gift in Jesus Christ our Lord.

S. P. T. Prideaux

Founder's Day and other occasions

(189) O eternal God, the resurrection and the life of all that believe in thee, who art always to be praised, as well in the dead as in the living: we give thee hearty thanks for thy servant . . . our founder (*or* thy servants our benefactors), by whose bounty we are

here brought up to godliness and the studies of good learning, beseeching thee that we, well using all these thy blessings to the praise and honour of thy holy name, may at length, together with him (them) and all thy servants departed this life, be brought to the immortal glory of the resurrection; through Jesus Christ our Lord.

Elizabethan, or earlier, used in many ancient collegiate foundations

Art and Letters

(190) O God, who by thy Spirit in our hearts dost lead men to desire thy perfection, to seek for truth, and to rejoice in beauty; illumine, we pray thee, and inspire all thinkers, writers, artists and craftsmen; that in whatsoever is true and pure and lovely, thy name may be hallowed and thy kingdom come on earth; through Jesus Christ our Lord.

Book of Common Order

(191) Direct and bless, we beseech thee, Lord, those who speak where many listen, and write what many read; that they may do their part in making the heart of the people wise, its mind sound, and its will righteous; to the honour of Jesus Christ our Lord.

Book of Common Order

Home and Children

(192) O God, who hast bidden us to honour our parents, and who by thy Son, our Saviour, hast

sanctified the life of home: bless, we beseech thee, with thy gracious protection, all those who are related to me; keep them in health and safety; help me lovingly to fulfil my duty to them, and knit us closely together in love and worship of thee; through the same Jesus Christ our Lord.

(193) Heavenly Father, after whom all fatherhood in heaven and earth is named: bless, we beseech thee, all children, and give to their parents and to all in whose charge they may be, thy spirit of wisdom and love: so that the home in which they grow up may be to them an image of thy kingdom, and the care of their parents a likeness of thy love; through Jesus Christ our Lord.

Prayers of the World-Wide Church

The Suffering, Sick and Unhappy

(194) We bring before thee, O Lord, the troubles and perils of peoples and nations, the sighing of prisoners and captives, the sorrows of the bereaved, the necessities of strangers, the helplessness of the weak, the despondency of the weary, the failing powers of the aged. O Lord, draw near to each, for the sake of Jesus Christ our Lord.

St. Anselm (12th Century)

(195) Almighty God, whose blessed Son Jesus Christ went about doing good, and healing all manner of sickness and all manner of disease among the people: continue, we beseech thee, this his gracious work

among us, especially in our hospitals, and dispensaries; cheer, heal and sanctify the sick; grant to doctors and nurses wisdom and skill, sympathy and patience; and assist with thy blessing all who are seeking to prevent suffering and to forward thy purposes of love; through Jesus Christ our Lord.

War Prayer (1914-1918)

(196) Grant, O Lord, to all those who are bearing pain, thy spirit of healing, thy spirit of life, thy spirit of peace and hope, of courage and endurance. Cast out from them the spirit of anxiety and fear; grant them perfect confidence and trust in thee, that in thy light they may see light; through Jesus Christ our Lord.

Prayers of the World-Wide Church

COLLECTS FOR THE GREAT SEASONS

Advent

(197) Almighty God, give us grace that we may cast away the works of darkness, and put upon us the armour of light, now in the time of this mortal life, in which thy Son Jesus Christ came to visit us in great humility; that in the last day, when he shall come again in his glorious majesty to judge both the quick and the dead, we may rise to the life immortal; through him who liveth and reigneth with thee and the Holy Ghost, now and ever.

Book of Common Prayer

Saint Andrew's Day

(198) Almighty God, who didst give such grace unto thy holy apostle Saint Andrew, that he readily obeyed the calling of thy son Jesus Christ, and followed him without delay: grant unto us all that we, being called by thy holy word, may forthwith give up ourselves obediently to fulfil thy holy commandments; through the same Jesus Christ our Lord.

Book of Common Prayer

Christmas

(199) Almighty God, who didst wonderfully create man in thine own image, and didst yet more wonder-

fully restore him: grant, we beseech thee, that as thy Son, our Lord Jesus Christ, was made in the likeness of men, so we may be made partakers of thy divine nature; through the same thy Son, who with thee and the Holy Ghost liveth and reigneth one God, world without end.

Book of Common Prayer (1928)

Epiphany

(200) O God, who by the shining of a star didst guide the wise men to behold thy Son, our Lord; show us thy heavenly light, and give us grace to follow until we find him, and, finding him rejoice; through the same Jesus Christ our Lord.

Book of Common Order

Ash Wednesday and Lent

(201) Almighty and everlasting God, who hatest nothing that thou hast made, and dost forgive the sins of all them that are penitent: create and make in us new and contrite hearts, that we worthily lamenting our sins, and acknowledging our wretchedness, may obtain of thee, the God of all mercy, perfect remission and forgiveness; through Jesus Christ our Lord.

Book of Common Prayer

Palm Sunday

(202) Almighty and everlasting God, who, of thy tender love towards mankind, hast sent thy Son, our Saviour Jesus Christ, to take upon him our flesh, and to suffer death upon the cross, that all mankind should

follow the example of his great humility: mercifully grant, that we may both follow the example of his patience, and also be made partakers of his resurrection; through the same Jesus Christ our Lord.

Book of Common Prayer

Good Friday

(203) Almighty God, we beseech thee graciously to behold this thy family, for which our Lord Jesus Christ was contented to be betrayed, and given up into the hands of wicked men, and to suffer death upon the cross, who now liveth and reigneth with thee and the Holy Ghost, ever one God, world without end.

Book of Common Prayer

Easter

(204) O God, who for our redemption didst give thine only-begotten Son to the death of the cross, and by his glorious resurrection hast delivered us from the power of our enemy; grant us so to die daily unto sin, that we may evermore live with him in the joy of his resurrection; through the same Jesus Christ our Lord.

Book of Common Prayer (1928)

Ascension Day

(205) Grant, we beseech thee, almighty God, that like as we do believe thy only-begotten Son our Lord Jesus Christ to have ascended into the heavens; so we may also in heart and mind thither ascend, and with him continually dwell, who liveth and reigneth with thee and the Holy Ghost, one God, world without end.

Book of Common Prayer

Whitsunday

(206) God, who as at this time didst teach the hearts of thy faithful people, by sending to them the light of thy Holy Spirit: grant us by the same Spirit to have a right judgment in all things, and evermore to rejoice in his holy comfort; through the merits of Christ Jesus our Saviour, who liveth and reigneth with thee, in the unity of the same Spirit, one God, world without end.

Book of Common Prayer

All Saints' Day

(207) O almighty God, who hast knit together thine elect in one communion and fellowship, in the mystical body of thy Son Christ our Lord: grant us grace so to follow thy blessed saints in all virtuous and godly living, that we may come to those unspeakable joys, which thou hast prepared for them that unfeignedly love thee; through Jesus Christ our Lord.

Book of Common Prayer

RESPONSORIES

Adoration and Thanksgiving

(208) *V.* Praise the Lord, O my soul,
R. And all that is within me praise his holy name.

(209) *V.* Praise the Lord, O my soul,
R. And forget not all his benefits.

(210) *V.* Let us bless the Lord.
R. Thanks be to God.

(211) *V.* O give thanks unto the Lord for he is gracious
R. And his mercy endureth for ever.

Confession and Forgiveness

(212) *V.* O Saviour of the World, who by thy Cross and precious Blood hast redeemed us,
R. Save us and help us, we humbly beseech thee, O Lord.

(213) *V.* O Lamb of God that takest away the sins of the world,
R. Have mercy on us.

(214) *V.* Make me a clean heart, O God,
R. *And renew a right spirit within me.*

(215) *V.* Show us thy mercy, O Lord,
R. *And grant us thy salvation.*

(216) Lord, have mercy upon us.
Christ, have mercy upon us.
Lord, have mercy upon us.

Acts of Faith

(217) *V.* Lord we believe;
R. *Help thou our unbelief.*

(218) *V.* Our help standeth in the name of the Lord
R. *Who hath made heaven and earth.*

Petition and Intercession

(219) *V.* Holy Father, hear us,
R. *Through Jesus Christ our Lord.*

(220) *V.* Graciously hear us, O Christ.
R. *Graciously hear us, O Lord Christ.*

(221) *V.* O Lord, let thy mercy be shewed upon us
R. *As we do put our trust in thee.*

(222) SOME ARROW PRAYERS

On rising

Lord, thou knowest how busy I must be this day; if I forget thee do not thou forget me. *J. Astley*

On bathing

Wash me throughly from my wickedness; and cleanse me from my sins.

On eating

For every cup and plateful, God make me truly grateful.

On opening the Bible

Help me, for I am thine; I study thy precepts.

Psalm 119. 94

On entering the library or classroom

Send out thy light and thy truth; let them lead me.

On entering the Union or cafeteria

Preserve me, O Lord, from idle gossip which profits nothing.

On entering a hospital

Lord, help me to remember that there are no diseases, but only sick people.

On facing a class

Lord, let me not cause one of these little ones to stumble.

In sudden temptation

Lord, help me to be master of myself, that I may be the servant of others.

On going to bed

The Lord shall light my candle, and make my darkness to be light.

On adjusting the calendar or diary

Lord, teach me to number my days, that I may apply my heart unto wisdom.

DEDICATION OF OFFERING

(223) Blessed be thou, O Lord God, for ever and ever. Thine, O Lord, is the greatness, and the power, and the victory, and the majesty; for all that is in the heaven and in the earth is thine. Thine is the kingdom, O Lord, and thou art exalted as head above all. Both riches and honour come of thee, and of thine own do we now give thee, for the good of thy Church and the glory of thy name; through Jesus Christ our Lord.

Accept, Lord Jesus, these offerings which we bring thee with our love. Follow them with thy blessing, that they may speak of thee to whoever may enjoy them. For thine own love's sake we ask it.

CLOSING OF SERVICES

(224) Almighty God, who hast given us grace at this time with one accord to make our common supplications unto thee; and dost promise, that when two or three are gathered together in thy name thou wilt grant their requests: Fulfil now, O Lord, the desires and petitions of thy servants, as may be most expedient for them; granting us in this world knowledge of thy truth, and in the world to come life everlasting.

St. Chrysostom (Book of Common Prayer)

(225) We commend unto thee, O Lord,
our souls and our bodies,
our minds and our thoughts,
our prayers and our hopes,
our health and our work,
our life and our death;
our parents and brothers and sisters,
our benefactors and friends,
our neighbours, our countrymen,
and all Christian folk
this day and always.

Bishop Lancelot Andrewes (17th Century)

(226) To God the Father, who loved us, and made us accepted in the Beloved:
To God the Son, who loved us, and loosed us from our sins by his own blood:

To God the Holy Spirit, who sheddeth the love of God abroad in our hearts:
To the one true God be all love and all glory for time and for eternity. *Bishop Ken*

(227) Love eternal,
Love that sufferest long and still art kind,
Love that seekest not thine own,
Love that believest in us,
Love that hopest in us,
Love that bearest with us,
Love that never failest,
Love that abidest and shalt abide,
Lover that art in all things and over all things,
God, immortal, invisible,
Creator, Redeemer, Sanctifier.
Thou reignest,
And in thee is our trust and hope,
Now and for evermore.
The Kingdom, the Power and the Glory

(228) Unto the Father, and unto the Son, and unto the Holy Spirit, be ascribed in the Church all honour and glory, might, majesty, dominion, and blessing, now, henceforth, and for ever.

(229) Sanctify, O Lord, both our coming in and our going forth; and grant that when we leave thy house we may not leave thy presence, but be thou ever near unto us and keep us near unto thee, through Jesus Christ our Lord. *R. Ambrose Reeves* (1929)

(230) BENEDICTIONS

The grace of our Lord Jesus Christ, and the love of

God, and the fellowship of the Holy Ghost, be with *us* all evermore. *II Cor. 13. 14*

The peace of God, which passeth all understanding, keep *our* hearts and minds in the knowledge of God and of his Son Jesus Christ our Lord. *Phil. 4. 7*

And the blessing of God Almighty, the Father, the Son and the Holy Ghost, be amongst *us* and remain with *us* always.

The God of hope fill *us* with all joy and peace in believing, that *we* may abound in hope, in the power of the Holy Ghost. *Rom. 15. 13*

May the blessing of God Almighty, the Father, the Son, and the Holy Spirit, rest upon *us* and upon all *our* work and worship done in his name. May he give *us* light to guide us, courage to support *us*, and love to unite *us*, now and for evermore.

The Kingdom, the Power and the Glory

Unto God's gracious mercy and protection we commit *ourselves*. The Lord bless *us* and keep *us*. The Lord make his face to shine upon *us* and be gracious unto *us*. The Lord lift up the light of his countenance upon *us*, and give *us* peace, both now and for evermore.

Grace, mercy, and peace from God the Father, Son, and Holy Spirit, be with *us* henceforth and for ever.

Go in peace; God the Father, Son, and Holy Spirit bless, preserve, and keep *us* this day (night) and for evermore.

ACKNOWLEDGMENTS

We wish to record our grateful thanks to the following authors and owners of copyright for permission to make use of prayers:

Lady Sykes for two prayers by the late Dr. Percy Dearmer; the Very Rev. E. Milner White, Dean of York, Canon G. W. Briggs, and the Oxford University Press for prayers from *Daily Prayer* and for directing our attention to a number of ancient non-copyright prayers; the Society of the Sacred Mission, Kelham, for a prayer from *New Every Morning*; the Oxford University Press for prayers from *The Kingdom, the Power and the Glory* and from *The Book of Common Order of the Church of Scotland*; Messrs. Basil Blackwell and Mott, Ltd., Oxford, for a prayer by the Rev. A. Campbell Fraser from *A Book of Prayers*; Messrs. Longmans, Green and Co., Ltd., for prayers from *Mysteries of the Mass* by Father Roche and from *Prayers for the City of God*; Messrs. J. M. Dent and Sons, Ltd., for a prayer from *The Free Church Book of Common Prayer*; the Bishop of Sheffield for prayers by the late John Hunter; the Rev. Canon S. P. T. Prideaux, D.D.; the Provost and Authorities of King's College, Cambridge, for two prayers; the Society for the Propagation of the Gospel for prayers from *Prayers of the World-Wide Church*;

the Principal of Westcott House, Cambridge, and Messrs. W. Heffer and Sons, Ltd., for a litany from *A Simple Form of Compline*; Dr. Reinhold Niebuhr; Messrs. Macmillan and Co., Ltd., and the Rev. A. Westcott, for prayers by the late Bishop Westcott; the S.P.C.K. for prayers from *Occasional Prayers Reconsidered* and from *Prayers for Lambeth 1948*; Messrs. A. R. Mowbray for prayers from *Memorials upon Several Occasions*; the Bishop of Johannesburg for prayers from *Venite Adoremus*.

Extracts from the Prayer Book as proposed in 1928 have been reprinted in this publication by permission of the Prayer Book Copyright Committee of the Central Board of Finance of the Church of England.

Every effort has been made to trace the sources of the prayers. If any copyright has been unwittingly infringed, the pardon of the owner is begged. Acknowledgment will gladly be made in later editions.

THE NICENE CREED

I BELIEVE in one God the Father Almighty, Maker of heaven and earth, and of all things visible and invisible.

And in one Lord Jesus Christ, the only-begotten Son of God, Begotten of his Father before all worlds, God of God, Light of Light, Very God of very God, Begotten not made, Being of one substance with the Father, By whom all things were made: Who for us men and for our salvation came down from heaven, And was incarnate by the Holy Ghost of the Virgin Mary, And was made man, And was crucified also for us under Pontius Pilate. He suffered and was buried, And the third day he rose again according to the Scriptures, And ascended into heaven, And sitteth on the right hand of the Father. And he shall come again with glory to judge both the quick and the dead: Whose kingdom shall have no end.

And I believe in the Holy Ghost, The Lord and giver of life, Who proceedeth from the Father and the Son, Who with the Father and the Son together is worshipped and glorified, Who spake by the Prophets. And I believe one Catholick and Apostolick Church. I acknowledge one Baptism for the remission of sins. And I look for the Resurrection of the dead, And the life of the world to come.